BRAIN to BANK

How to Get Your Idea Out of Your Head and Cash In

DORINE RIVERS
PhD, PMP

ALPHA 81 INC.

FIRST EDITION

Rivers, Dorine. Brain to Bank/written by
Dorine Rivers
Library of Congress Control Number 2022917769
ISBN: 978-0-9728322-0-5
Non-Fiction/Business

The individuals and companies portrayed in this book are real.
All names have been changed to maintain confidentiality.
Use your imagination... surely you know people and companies
just like the ones mentioned. Don't be them. Be yourself:
A successful entrepreneur who has learned what to do and what not to do.

www.BraintoBank.com
www.Smartz.Academy

Published by Alpha 81 Publishing
Carefree, Arizona

This book is dedicated to my five children
Jason, Emily, Joshua, Jacob, and Babe,
all of whom have the guts to dare mighty things
and transform hard goals and ambitious dreams into reality.
You are all my heroes and I want to be just like you when I grow up.

"Far better it is to dare mighty things, to win glorious triumphs, even though checkered by failure, than to take rank with those poor spirits who neither enjoy much nor suffer much, because they live in the gray twilight that knows neither victory nor defeat."

—Theodore Roosevelt

FREE RESOURCES

I have a plethora of resources and tools that will help you get your idea from brain to bank. I am forever searching for the latest and greatest roadmaps, websites, templates, checklists, guides, and strategies that will make it possible for you to create, market, and sell your product or service.

With these additional resources, you'll be able to improve and accelerate getting your idea out of your head and cash in even quicker. Some of these resources include:

- The complete resources mentioned in the book, including links
- Downloadable product development roadmaps, including one for FDA products
- A comprehensive project management template
- Business plan checklist
- Customer avatar template
- Distributor avatar template
- Outsourcing guides and links
- Survey guides and links
- And much more

To download these free resources, scan the QR code below or go to www.BrainToBank.com/Resources.

CONTENTS

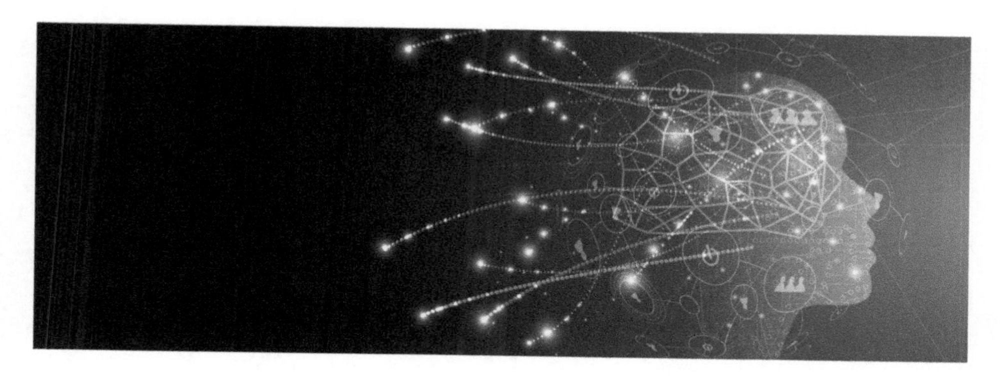

BRAIN TO BANK™

HOW TO GET YOUR IDEA OUT OF YOUR HEAD AND CASH IN

PREFACE

This book is designed for individuals, partnerships, and corporations who already have an idea for a product or service. You're not looking for ideas, because the one you have has been rattling around in your head for a really long time and is desperate to break out into the real world.

Your idea is well seasoned, you know exactly what it will be, and you already know if you need to build it on a SaaS platform, create a stand-alone product, manufacture it, and/or create a prototype to see if it works.

You are reading this book because you're ready to go from *Brain to Bank*.

You're ready to take the next steps to get your product or service into the hands of consumers and you'll do whatever it takes to get it there.

This book will serve as your "pit crew," supporting you at every turn. I'm yelling and screaming for you to keep driving, go the distance, and cross the finish line as a winner.

Ladies and Gentlemen, start your engines!

INTRODUCTION

Brain to Bank is intended for anyone who has an idea revving up in their brain that just won't let go until it sees the light of day and *cha chings!* in their bank account after being strategically driven to the finish line.

Getting Your Idea Out of Your Head and Cashing In

No matter what your product or service, no matter how brilliant you know your idea may be, the chain of events that will bring the idea to market usually follows a well-thought-out course of action.[1]

The beginning of such an adventure — and it is just that, an adventure—may spring from an event. It may appear as a plausible solution to a problem while you're working in the office. It could come from conversations with peers and associates.

Or it may crawl out of your brain's frontal cortex at 3 a.m. and sound like this:

"Yeah, I've got a really awesome idea for a really cool product that will change the ______________________________

(fill in the blank according to your revelation)

industry forever and I'm going to create it and save the world!
Oh…and get really rich, too!"

As you dive into what it takes to make the idea happen, and learn about things you didn't know existed, a number of questions may keep you up at night:

- How do I know someone isn't already secretly working on this and will beat me to the market?
- I know my idea is worth billions of dollars. How do I convince investors?
- Where do I find an investor who will recognize the genius of it all?
- Do I need a strategic partner to help market my product, and where do I find one? For that matter, how do you define "strategic"?
- How do I get endorsements? I just figured out that rejection can make or break the success of my product. If my product or service is difficult to use,

or if professionals don't believe in the efficacy of the product or device, it won't get used, and ultimately, they will stop purchasing it. What do I do?

- My idea is so awesome that a company will want to buy my company right now. What is it worth? How do I do this so I can get on with my life on the beaches of Costa Rica?

And on and on and on.

Maybe it's a great idea, or maybe it's not.

Why not?

Because recognizing and developing well-targeted, innovative products and solutions and bringing them to market on schedule and within budget is complicated. You may have a really great idea, but do you know how to get it into the hands of others so they can benefit from your brilliance?

This book fills in the gaps between what you know, what you don't know, and, most importantly, what you don't know you don't know, so you can *finally* see your brainchild come to life.

The processes and systems needed from initial concept to product development, and ultimately to the end-use of your product, follow a well-designed blueprint that will be your guide, so you'll know what to do, why you're doing it, how to do it, with whom, and when.

It is estimated that 30,000 new products go from concept to commercialization every year.[2] Your idea could be one of those 30,000. Why not your product? Take your turn. Your number's up!

Tell Your Fear of Failure to Take a Leap

Ten years ago, I attended a self-improvement seminar in the mountains of Northern California. The week-long agenda included outdoor exercises designed to challenge your fears. One challenge was to climb an old, 50-foot-high wooden telephone pole equipped with metal brackets as footholds.

The objective was to reach the highest point of the pole, stand on the very top with nothing to hold onto, stand there for a full minute while the pole swayed side-to-side in the wind, and then leap out and grab the steel bar of a trapeze 10 feet out. Having spent my youth climbing trees and leaping off riverbank cliffs 30 feet above the water, I thought the challenge was no big deal.

As I watched others climb toward the top of the pole and then stop just short of the last step, I began to wonder if it was as easy as it looked. I realized that as I reached the top of the pole, where there was nothing to grab hold of to pull myself up, I would have to climb the last 14 inches with sheer muscle and grit, and quickly bring my other foot up for balance.

I watched as one, and then another climber got stuck before making that final step. One woman sat on the topmost rung for over an hour trying to muster up her courage to go on. Shouts of encouragement echoed from below. Still, she couldn't make herself move. Finally, she climbed back down the pole… defeated.

Several others got just as far, only to fail and climb back down.

Then it was my turn.

Geared up in a hard hat and harness attached to a wire as a safety device, I started climbing. It felt easy until I was about midway and the pole began to sway in the wind. The farther up I went, the more it rocked back and forth.

Gripping the metal rungs even harder, I kept climbing.

Finally, I was on the last rung… the place where others had been and had stopped and then turned back. I vowed I would not do that. I sat with my foot on the last rung for about a minute, and then I counted to three. 1…2…3… and made myself lift my left foot up onto the top of the pole. I was almost there.

I paused. I realized I would have to use every ounce of muscle and grit to finish the climb and get my other foot onto the top of the pole. With nothing to hold on to. Just me up there… depending on just me.

And then it also occurred to me that the worst thing that could happen was that I'd fall and have to climb back up and try it again.

So, I put all of my weight on my left foot and lifted my right onto the top of the swaying pole. I stood there amazed I hadn't fallen. I basked in the glory of it all for a few minutes, taking in the glorious landscape that I could see for miles around me.

"Waaaaaaah hooooooo!!" I shouted.

And then I took the big leap for the trapeze bar.

Oh, what a feeling of success that was!

Don't be the person who climbs back down. Don't sit there clinging to the footholds deciding if you're going to take the last step. Decide before you climb that you'll go all out and not quit until you make it. Keep going while you have the momentum of climbing up rung by rung. One "rung victory" at a time. The last step is part of the momentum you already have. Take it! Do it! 1… 2… 3… Go!

Then you'll be standing on the very top spreading your arms out wide, taking in the incredible beauty of having made it and shouting, "Waaaaaaah hooooooo!!"

You Are the Success Story

Most courses and books have great stories about people who have succeeded and made it all happen. I like these stories because they are usually true and I feel motivated and inspired by them.

But another reaction to these success stories is wondering not if you, too, will know what to do when your chance comes, but if you'll also know what not to do. My experience in life and business has been that I have learned much more from what didn't work and from mistakes I made, then from things that went smoothly. If it's true you learn from your mistakes, then I must be the smartest person in the world!

The good news is you personally don't have to make all those mistakes. You can be smart from the get-go and learn from the errors of others. Oliver Wendell Holmes once said, "Learn from the mistakes of others ... You can't live long enough to make them all yourself!"

As you read the section in this book titled **Another Episode in the Entrepreneur Drama Series *I Didn't See It Coming***, take each lesson, learn from it, and skip the pain of making the mistake by following the "do this instead."

Then you really will be one of the smartest people in the world.

ADVICE FROM INDUSTRY EXPERTS

Everything in life is a collaboration, right from the birth of little ole you up until now. If you've read Malcolm Gladwell's book *Outliers,* you learned that genius is overrated. Success is not just about innate ability but instead is merged with other key factors, such as opportunity, meaningful hard work (10,000 hours to gain mastery), and your cultural legacy.

I have a dozen or more things I want to do and learn well but I don't have 10,000 hours to devote to each one. I discovered the next best thing is to rely on the masters. I find experts in the things I want to know about, and I collaborate with them to absorb and acquire specific knowledge. As you advance through this book, you'll get to learn from these experts, too.

I have been lucky my entire life. I am the person that finds the four-leaf clover in a big meadow, stumbles upon an opportunity flitting by just in time to seize it, or throws the ring onto the soda pop bottle in the Magic Mountain arcade and takes home a stuffed lion bigger than the motor home we came in. So, it's no surprise I have found some of the brightest experts in their fields to contribute knowledge and advice in this book.

Because I value not only the advice of my experts, but their personalities and writing styles as well, their words and unique ways of conveying their expert advice has been left unaltered. So, if you see an alphabetical number, a roman numeral, or other inconsistent design elements to what I have used throughout this book, it's because you are experiencing each expert's individual writing style.

I share my experts with you. Learn well, my friend.

The Thirty-Something Club

A Special Note for those of you who wonder if you're too old to jump in on the action of bringing your idea into the marketplace:

Some of you may be honorary members of the Thirty-Something Club.
There are no membership fees; you've already paid your dues.

The Thirty-Something Club originated years ago when the first few of my 20 grandkids were under the age of seven. One day they asked me, "How old are you, Mammy?" Knowing they weren't able to do much addition yet, I responded, "I'm thirty-twenty-one."

That seemed to satisfy them... and me. I have been thirty-something ever since.

Now that I'm in the Thirty-Something Club, I invite anyone in this distinguished league to view it as just that... distinguished, laced with experience, wisdom, and plenty to offer. Yes, taking your idea from brain to bank is for you too. Maybe even more so now that you've got the smartz and experience to really knock it out of the park.

A post on LinkedIn says it all:

"I get tired of "under 40" lists. Show me someone who got their Ph.D. at 60 after losing everything. Give me the 70-year-old debut novelist who writes from a lifetime of love and grief. Give me calloused hands and tender hearts."
~ Doug Murano, Strategic Communicator, Writer, and Educator

Gray hair (or no hair) be damned.

Embrace your brilliance and experience and get going after it!

How This Book is Organized

This book has 17 chapters that include information and resources so you will know what to do and when to do it. Complete the chapters in order. If you do one per day you will finish the book in less than 2.5 weeks. Yes, I'm a math genius.

Obviously, you can do more than one a day if you're gung-ho and on a panting, throbbing quest to learn as much as you can as fast as possible. This is my personal, preferred method since I turn into a raving lunatic, jumping the gun at the starting line, when I'm overly excited about a project, which is most of the time. But then I have to take a step back and take time to organize my thoughts and my action plan.

When you're bootstrapping it and working on getting a company up via the DIY method, nothing matters more than creating action steps to reach your milestones. Put on your meanest, power-driving boots, buckle yourself in, and get ready to roar through the miles of getting your idea from brain to bank.

ROADMAP MILEAGE

At the end of each chapter, you will be prompted to take action on items NOW to keep driving your idea from mind to market, in the sections titled Action Accelerators.

As you work – yes, work – your way through this book you will gain the knowledge, skills, tools, and confidence to see your fabuloso idea all the way through from concept to completion.

Critical to this journey is applying what you have learned in action steps that will get you closer to the finished product. When products fail to launch, it's usually not because the idea was bad and couldn't be executed, but because it wasn't fully/strategically executed. It's important to take your thoughts about your product or service and convert them into action steps. Otherwise, what's the point of reading this book or continuing to dream about an idea that will never see the light of day?

So, take your thoughts about what to do, move them into action steps, and then do them, all of them. No good thought or idea means anything without action. Action leads to results.

If you're the type of person who has a strong inclination to action, then no worries, you will do what you always do... take action.

If you're someone who needs a mentor, coach, or others to light a fire underneath you and keep you on track, then implement this needed external motivation and keep it in play until you have achieved your goal.

This book will transform your inspired idea into something of value if you complete the steps strategically outlined for you and do them one by one.

Yes, it's a big elephant, but just munch those tiny bites one at a time and you'll get there. I've done it dozens of times. So can you.

Please note there is an extensive glossary in the back of this book. Please consult it as needed so you can fully comprehend the concepts as you THINK IT, ORGANIZE IT, and DO IT.

After completing this book you'll have the knowledge and processes needed for implementation, coupled with the ability and desire to take the necessary action to get your idea out of your head and into the marketplace, and cash in.

Now grab your helmet, head onto the track, and let's get headed down the road to success.

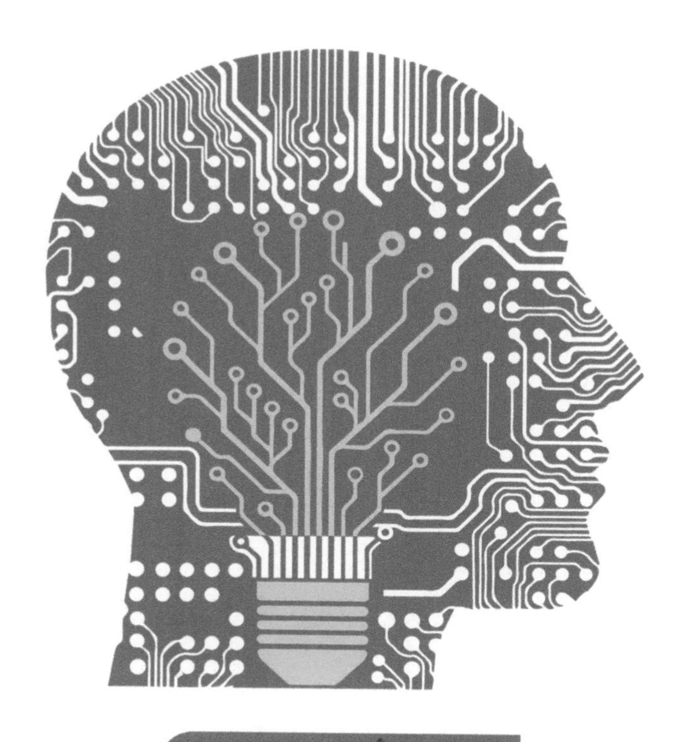

PART ONE

LADIES AND GENTLEMEN, START YOUR ENGINES

Chapter 1

Know Your Why

THE BIG CHEESE

By the time I was 26 years old, I had five babies.

I know, I know, you're going to quote my father-in-law, who upon hearing we were pregnant with number five responded, "Don't you know you can just do it for fun?"

I'll tell you what's not fun: I had my fifth baby at midnight, in the rain, in the front seat of a Volkswagen. Who knew that the VW front passenger seats were so versatile?

When I took my number five baby home, my oldest child was five years old. Yeah, I know, you can do the math: one kid a year for five years.

Here's more math: zero times zero always equals zero. And that's how much money we had.

We did, however, have a nice patch of dirt in our backyard. So, I planted a garden. I also begged my neighbors to please oh please let me pick the fruit from their unattended trees: apples, pears, cherries, apricots, plums, whatever. I didn't care as long as I could reach the fruit and pick it, even from a 20-foot ladder.

Then I canned and bottled more than 1,000 jars of fruit and vegetables from the garden, and made salsa, pickles, jams, jellies, and whatever else I could figure out, so we'd have food. I even pureed fruits and vegetables in a blender and made my own baby food.

It wasn't enough. I needed money. Hard, cold cash. You can't pay the mortgage with applesauce and you can't trade pickles for your electric bill.

I kept asking myself, *What else can I do? How can I stay at home with my five kids and help us survive?*

I investigated a few options, but week after week yielded nothing. Until I discovered...

A small fresh cheese manufacturer out of Loa, Utah.

They sold wholesale cheese products to anyone who wanted to sign up as a distributor.

I signed up the same day.

Then I set out to make phone calls to everyone I knew. I even called people I didn't know from neighborhood directories I confiscated from block parties and churches. I strategically took phone orders during daily nap time.

Once a week I'd drive to the local walk-in refrigerated cheese facility and get the cheeses on my delivery list. I'd buy wholesale and then sell retail to my customers and collect the difference.

Classic business model, right?

Except I had five minor partners to take with me to the walk-in refrigerator and on my deliveries. While the three middle kids (ages 1½, 3 and 4) squirmed, squabbled, and whined because it was all too long, too hot, and too boring in the car, my oldest child, the 5-year-old, delivered cheese orders to the front door of each house while I literally nursed my baby in the driver's seat of the car.

That oldest son would return with cash or a check for $5.14, which netted us about $2.00, and then we'd drive to the next house on the delivery list.

One inherent problem of my Big Cheese business was that I was not just the Big Cheese — I was the only Cheese. I was trapped doing all of the work myself since I was the sole employee. If I didn't go to the walk-in cooler and get the cheese every week, if I didn't deliver the cheese every week, if I didn't continually call every week to get the next orders, I didn't get paid.

One sweltering August afternoon, I piled my five little kids into our clunky, wood-paneled station wagon to make our deliveries. Before the first delivery stop, we ran out of gas. Yep, just like in the movies. There I was on the side of a busy highway with five kids 5 years old and younger in a car that wouldn't budge. Now, you have to remember this was waaaaaay before cell phones, so I had to gather my chicks into a tight flock and go find some gas. We walked. And walked. And walked.

I remember being scared to death of the traffic on the highway, so I kept them to the shoulder huddled in a body-hugging clutch while I walked nearest to the road carrying two of them, one in each arm, all the while making sure the other three were holding hands and making progress.

We finally reached a gas station where I found an empty, plastic, one-gallon milk container in a trash barrel. I rinsed it out and filled it with gas with the last dollar I had.

And then we walked back. Everyone was crying... including me.

I barely had enough gas to finish our deliveries before coasting into the driveway of our home with five exhausted children.

This can't be my life, I thought.

I had to figure something out. I couldn't keep doing this.

What were my options?

1. Go to work for someone else.
   Shoot me now.
2. I could buy a fast-food franchise and run it by managing employees. Except a franchise would require money. Nix the franchise idea.
3. I could take some of my ideas and take them from brain to bank. If I did it right, I wouldn't need a bunch of cash. Just lots of sweat equity, grit, determination, and a moxie attitude that wouldn't quit. All while working from home. Perfect.

So, I created a new business model for the cheese business; one corporate hadn't considered. I created mini-franchises where I would set up businesses for other mothers to buy and deliver the cheese in well-established territories. The territory was theirs for the taking if they picked up the cheese and delivered it to a designated neighborhood.

I negotiated with the *head cheese* of the corporation to give me a percentage of all territories I set up and maintained. I soon had a dozen franchisees, all manageable from my small kitchen desk.

I had taken my mini-franchise idea from brain to bank, and it had paid off.

My *Why* was I needed to support my kids, and I also wanted to be home with them. My *Why* got me up in the morning, on the phone, making sure all of my franchisees were running their businesses properly. My *Why* created a vision and blueprint for a successful business because I believed in it, and I never quit trying to make it happen.

Your *Why* won't be just about making money. It'll be bigger than that. Dig deep and find the *real Why*. It will be so compelling you won't be able to deny the drive it gives you to start, keeping going, and ultimately bring your product or service into the marketplace.

What is Your *Why*?

Your *Why* is about purpose, cause, and concept/idea. In his book *Start With Why,*[3] Simon Sinek says begin with the vision (the *Why*), then move to implementation (the "How"), and then master the product or service (the "What"). Most entrepreneurs begin by focusing on *what* they need to do and *how* they will do it instead of becoming crystal clear on *why* they want to do it.

The ***Why*** stems from your core purpose, the reason you get out of bed in the morning.

Your ***How*** explains the ways your product or service is unique and why others will want it.

Your ***What*** is the product or service itself.

Your customers will not be buying what you do, they will be buying *why* you are doing it.

Follow your passion and create a vision of what your finished product or service will look like. The real reason for *Why* will come from looking inside yourself and figuring out how your purpose can lead you where you want to go. Do what inspires you. The rest will follow.

Your *Why* may be as simple as being able to support yourself or your family. Or it could be something on a much grander scale, such as wanting to create a sustainable water solution for African desert countries and save millions of lives or develop a new medical device that brings down the death rate for diabetes patients. Whatever the *Why*, it will incite emotion and passion in you when you explain your idea to others.

When you figure out the root reason *Why* you want to bring your product or service to fruition, your passion and vision will give you the fuel you need to keep going until you have succeeded.

When you know your Why, what you do has meaning and purpose and moves you toward success in creating your product.

Whatever your *Why*, know what it is so it can propel you to the finish line.

Yes, you're going to hit deep, scary potholes on your road trip, encounter the flat tires of people not doing what they said they would do, get "rained on" by competitors, and maybe drive into a loud and flashing financial thunderstorm in the darkness. This is where you fiercely cling to your *Why* and ride it out... because you can. And you will. Your *Why* will see you through.

SIMPLE STEPS TO FIND YOUR *WHY*

"People don't buy what you do; they buy *why* you do it. And what you do simply proves what you believe."
— Simon Sinek, *Start with Why: How Great Leaders Inspire Everyone to Take Action*

If you've read this far, congratulations! Picking up a book about how to bring your idea to life in the competitive marketplace is one of the first steps in accomplishing your goals.

- ✓ *Check*

Feels good to tick off a to-do list item, right? Get ready for more. Throughout this book, you are going to break down those big, seemingly complicated processes into smaller pieces. As you complete each item, you'll continually find the motivation to ultimately cross the finish line.

One of the first steps in bringing your idea from brain to bank is to develop a strong sense of *Why.* Ask yourself:

- **Why** do I want to bring this idea to life?
- **Why** do I think it will be worth my time, effort, and money to develop and launch?
- **Why** do I think investors will want to invest money in developing my product?
- **Why** would anyone want to purchase my product?
- **Why** would anyone tell others about my product?

Coming up with the reasons behind why you are working to bring an idea to life can seem daunting. I can already hear your argument: *But I just wanted to do it, there isn't really much more to it.*

Unfortunately, your potential investors and future consumers can't read your mind to understand all that has gone into your decision to create, produce, and launch your product or service. They need to understand *Why* your product was brought to the market and how it can potentially solve a problem or meet a need they currently have.

If you can articulate your *why*, then you are well on your way to increasing the chance that your product will make it past the obstacles that stand in the way of its success.

Here's the good news: you can figure out your *Why* with a couple of simple steps:

Roadmap to Discovering Your *Why*

Are you ready to start getting down and dirty with figuring out *why* you are starting this process in the first place? Here are some questions you must answer if you are going to build a strong purpose for your idea, product, and business:

1. Why are you moving this idea from thought to action?

   If you are an entrepreneurial individual, you have probably already had millions of ideas pop up and disappear. *Why did this one stand out?* What makes it so special that it took up residency in your heart and mind over all other ideas?

2. What makes this idea stand out from other similar products or services on the market today?

   Are there any other similar products or services on the market like this one?

   If not, is there a reason why your idea hasn't been created yet?
   If there are, why do you believe your idea can rise above the competition?

3. Why would you spend money or give up a lucrative career to bring this idea to life?

To bring this concept into the real world, you are going to have to sacrifice time, energy, and financial resources to see it happen. Can you give a good answer as to *why* you are willing to give up other potential directions for your life or outcomes to see this idea go from brain to bank?

Confidence Is Key

These key questions intimidate entrepreneurs and thought leaders alike. They challenge who you are and why you do what you do every day. However, don't ignore the need to answer them. The more confidence you have in your *Why*, the better you will be able to navigate your project's inherent and inevitable challenges.

Confidence in your *Why* is your most important weapon in the process of bringing your idea from mind to market.

STAY IN YOUR ZONE OF GENIUS

From the Entrepreneur Drama Series *I Didn't See it Coming*

A few years ago, I worked with a company that had a core business of offering exotic cooking lessons in foreign countries complete with famous chefs and on-site wineries. Let's call them Global Cooking Adventures (GCA). After much success and decades of serving happy clients, GCA decided to venture out into the tech business and develop their own booking lessons platform to assist culinary entrepreneurs in growing their customer base and locations.

Ultimately this booking platform evolved to serve other companies in the culinary industry and provide other revenue streams. In time, GCA intended to sell the platform in an Initial Public Offering (IPO) or Mergers & Acquisitions (M&A) deal and retire rich on the beach of a remote Caribbean Island.

Cha ching! Cha ching! Cha ching!

Only it didn't turn out that way.

What this company failed to realize was that even though the booking platform was initially created to help acquire and retain business for their own company, it was not their core business. They were chefs, culinary instructors, and high-end restaurant food experts. They didn't know anything about SaaS and technology or managing domestic and remote platform programmers. They didn't know the difference between programming in Python, HTML, C++, C#, or any other musical alphabet coding.

They ran off the road and got stuck in a deep ditch because they took their eyes off their original expertise. They were distracted by the "shiny objects" luring them off their path. As Enzo, the wise-beyond-his-years dog and star of *The Art of Racing in the Rain,* is quick to remind us, "Your car goes where your eyes go."

IDENTIFY WORTHY IDEAS, INNOVATIONS, AND INVENTIONS

As you begin the process of defining your ideas, it's important to understand the differences between creativity, invention, and innovation.

Creativity is the ability to come up with new ideas or concepts. It has nothing to do with creating value or monetizing an idea.

Innovation is the process of creating value, that is, a new solution to an existing problem, and occurs when a need is identified and a product or service is developed to meet that need. Remember the cheese story? Innovators use existing technology in new ways. More on that in a minute.

Invention, on the other hand, creates new technology, a new way of doing something that can be proved different from, and usually superior to, previous technology or processes: the proverbial better mousetrap. This is what patents are made for, and filing an appropriate Intellectual Property (IP) patent(s) is of the utmost importance. Inventors are a creative bunch and usually have more ideas than they could ever bring to fruition.

After you have figured out whether your idea is an innovation or an invention, you'll have to identify what your potential consumers want and need, and then develop the idea into a product or service that meets those wants and needs. This is an initial step that must be completed before moving on to other steps in the process.

Another Episode in the Entrepreneur Drama Series
I Didn't See It Coming

I was hired as a consultant to a health and wellness company that lacked the vision to identify consumer needs. Instead of doing their homework and finding out what their customers wanted, they bulldozed ahead with what they wanted as founders.

They developed a line of products based on hype and anecdotal testimonies instead of scientific facts, relying on the promise of a high-level salesperson who swore she could make a market for them.

The company thought these products were unique, but because they were based on what the company itself wanted. The line's marketers had to try to create the need for them afterward by "selling" consumers the concept along with the products. Instead of customers getting products they did want and need and had impatiently awaited, they were bombarded with sales pitches loaded with reasons why they should buy products they hadn't wanted or needed.

But American consumers did not "buy into" the marketing of the products and the company's weak claims about them. As a result, the company was forced to pitch its new line overseas. It has been almost a decade since this company launched, and they still have very little traction in the U.S. market for their products.

A better approach would have been for the company to spend time and money on figuring out what health and wellness consumers in their niche market wanted and needed, and develop their product line accordingly. What a novel idea: find out first, and then deliver just what your customers want.

Paramount in moving your innovation or invention toward success is remembering that it will not be worth much if nobody wants to buy it.

Do your marketing homework first. Then you can play with development.

A FEW WORDS ABOUT EXPONENTIAL TECHNOLOGIES

Exponential technology is called exponential because it doubles in capability or performance within a given time period.

Exponential technologies include artificial intelligence (AI), augmented and virtual reality (AR, VR), data science, networks and computing systems, robotics, 3D printing, digital biology and biotech, medicine, nanotech, and digital fabrication, drones, and self-driving vehicles.

All of these exponential technologies are doubling consistently in capability and performance as Moore's Law predicts. Coined by Gordon Moore, the co-founder of Fairchild Semiconductor and CEO and co-founder of Intel, "Moore's law" is the observation that the number of transistors in a dense integrated circuit (IC) doubles about every two years. This law is based on an empirical relationship rather than on a law of physics.

Another fact about/principle of exponential technology is that its continually downward-adjusted price makes it possible to solve today's business problems more cheaply. The number of transistors goes up. The price goes down. Sweet. Here's an ancient story to help you better understand the concept of the word *exponential*:

Once upon a time there was a king in India who was an accomplished chess player. He loved to challenge visitors to a game of chess. One day a traveling sage was passing through the kingdom and was challenged by the king. The sage had played chess all his life with people from all over the world and gladly accepted the king's challenge. To motivate his opponent, the king offered any reward the sage could name. The sage modestly asked just for a few grains of rice in the following manner: the king was to place a single grain of rice on the first chess square and double it on every subsequent one. The king gladly accepted the sage's reward method.

After an intense match, to his astonishment the king lost the game of chess to the sage. Being a man of his word, he ordered a bag of rice to be brought to the chess board and began placing the grains according to the arrangement: one grain on the first square, two on the second, four on the third, eight on the fourth and so on.

As he watched the exponential growth of the rice payment, the king soon realized he would be unable to fulfill his promise. On the 20th square the king would have had to put 1,000,000 grains of rice. On the 40th square, the king would have had to put 1,000,000,000 grains of rice. And, finally, on the 64th square, the king would have placed 18,446,744,073,709,551,615 (eighteen quintillion four hundred forty-six quadrillion seven hundred forty-four trillion seventy-three billion seven hundred nine million five hundred fifty-one thousand six hundred fifteen) grains of rice. Ugh!

Seeing the king's dismay, the sage decided to be a nice guy and let him off the hook, and told him that he didn't have to pay the debt immediately, but could pay over time. The sage became the richest person in the world.

I don't tell you this story so you'll hire a chess coach and trick some billionaire who can't add (is that an oxymoron?) into agreeing to double rice grains in each of the 64 squares on a chessboard... payable in the form of hard, cold cash if he loses... but to illustrate the power of exponential technology and the exciting, continued advances made in many industries. If your brilliant idea includes exponential technology, you're in for an exciting ride!

FROM INDUSTRY EXPERTS

Key point: the "second half of the chessboard" is a phrase used in technology strategy. It was coined by Ray Kurzweil, author, entrepreneur, futurist, and inventor, who defines it as the point at which an exponentially growing factor begins to have a significant economic impact on an organization's overall business strategy.

In the chessboard example, while the number of grains on the first half of the chessboard is large, the amount on the second half is overwhelmingly (2^{32} > 4 billion times) larger.[4]

An illustration of the second half of Kurzweil's chessboard principle.[5] The letters are abbreviations for the SI metric prefixes.

1	2	4	8	16	32	64	128
256	512	1024	2048	4096	8192	16384	32768
65536	131K	262K	524K	1M	2M	4M	8M
16M	33M	67M	134M	268M	536M	1G	2G
4G	8G	17G	34G	68G	137G	274G	549G
1T	2T	4T	8T	17T	35T	70T	140T
281T	562T	1P	2P	4P	9P	18P	36P
72P	144P	288P	576P	1E	2E	4E	9E

If your invention includes exponential technology, plan on plenty of cash for IP, legal, and R&D. But also open that additional Wall Street brokerage account you've always wanted, because Moore's Law may very well turn out to be More's Law.

CHAPTER 1 - Action Accelerators

Take action on these items NOW to keep driving your idea from Brain to Bank:

1. Take some time to think about *why* you want to get your idea from brain to bank. Your *Why* is just that – yours. Once you have discovered the real reason (or reasons) you're willing to put in the needed effort and time, make sure it will motivate and sustain you throughout the process. If it won't, it's not your real *Why*, and you need to go back to the drawing board and figure it out.

   My *Why* for getting my idea from brain to bank is:

   ____

2. Write down five things you are good at in business.

   1) ____
   2) ____
   3) ____
   4) ____
   5) ____

3. How can you use these skills to bring your idea from brain to bank?

   ____

4. What potential "rabbit holes" should you avoid to help keep your focus in your Zone of Genius?

   ____

5. Identify whether your idea is an innovation or an invention. Explain why.

___

6. Write three things about your product or service that consumers either want or need and why.

___

7. What else might they want or need that could be a part of your product or service?

___

8. Why will they want to buy it?

___

9. Why will they want to buy it from YOU?

___

Chapter 2

Mapping Out Your Action Plan

WHAT'S INVOLVED IN THE DEVELOPMENT PROCESS

Several key components are involved in the stages and processes of any new product or service concept. Simplified, the path for the development of a new idea is Concept, Research, Development, Regulation, and Marketing.

To quote Ron Popeil of Ronco fame, "But wait, there's more!"

When you peel back the layers of the "I've got a killer idea" thought, things you need to know (and things you don't know you need to know) are gradually revealed. Soon, the process is far more complicated than you realized.

Two different flowcharts illustrate the process, one for a nonmedical, non-FDA-approved product or service, the other for a medical or FDA-approved product.

Whether used to create a new innovation, redesign an existing product (i.e., build a better mousetrap), or evaluate critical paths and bottlenecks to improve current systems and processes, the successful completion of the complexities of this entire progression will help to ensure the timely introduction of your product or service into the marketplace.

This is what a roadmap looks like for a nonmedical or non-FDA-approved product:

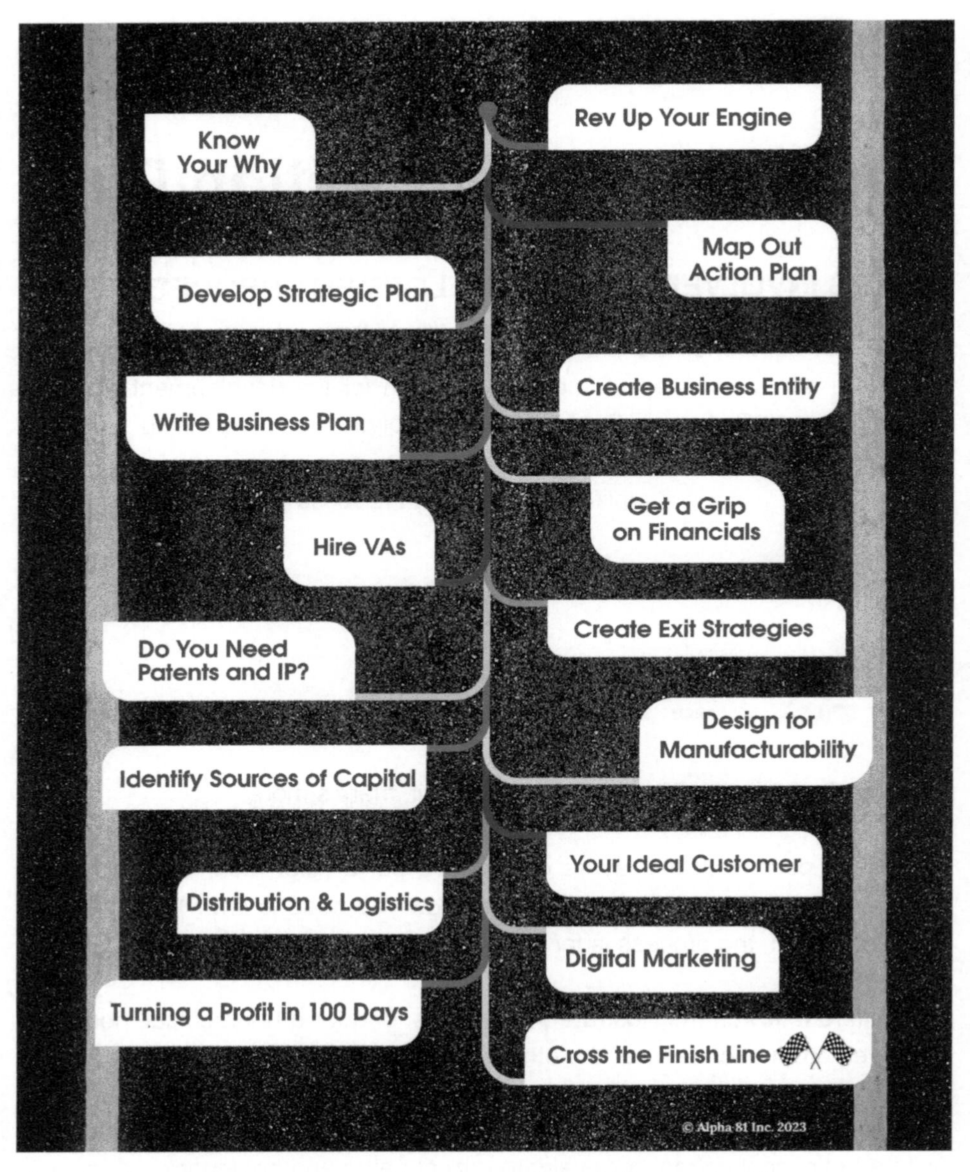

You can download this roadmap here: www.BrainToBank.com/Resources.

Check out the Appendix in this book for what a flow chart looks like for an FDA-approved product.

Before you slam this book shut, remember that we're going to break this process down into bite-size pieces.

Truly, don't sweat it. It will all be laid out for you like new clothes on the first day of school. You just need to go from step one to step two to step three... and do them in order.

BASS ACKWARDS

Another Episode in the Entrepreneur Drama Series
I Didn't See It Coming

Here's what can happen if you don't do things in order. A few years ago, I worked with a pharmaceutical company that had partnered with a medical device company to create a new product line that would be registered with the FDA for "professional use only" distribution. In other words, the products required a prescription from a licensed physician for someone to buy and use them.

The company formed an LLC. The partners all signed the Operating Agreement. The duties were divvied up, and they were off and running.

The products were developed, the manufacturing was rolling, and the packaging was created. The initial (but not final) FDA registrations were completed.

But then...

To get final FDA approval, the founders needed to prove the products were being manufactured according to FDA standards.

They were told that by abiding by ISO manufacturing standards at each step in the manufacturing process they would be safeguarding their products and this would lead to the required certification.

This meant every single step in the process had to meet ISO standards. The company completed ISO certification in this order:

- ✓ Packaging
- ✓ Manufacturing of product
- ✓ Step 4
- ✓ Step 3
- ✓ Step 2

  Step 1... uhhhhhh... Step 1 was not completed in a certifiable facility. And it never would be. The certification chain was broken. They should have discovered this first, not last.

Now what?

Because they had not adhered to the chain of certification required, they did not have the desired manufacturing outcome they needed. Just one step not in line with ISO certification standards meant the entire product was not certifiable.

These are the kinds of things you want to know before you get as far as manufacturing and packaging.

They had to scrap the entire line of products and the company. They were done. Over. *Fini*. Broke. The company was dissolved and buried in the "I Messed It Up" cemetery of business failures, leaving the founders with a loss of time and capital.

Had this company implemented the guidelines provided by ISO certification *at the beginning of the project* they would have been successful. If they had thought that far ahead, they would most likely still be in business today.

Even if your product will not require FDA approval, you want to know ahead of time where the potholes on the road might be so you can avoid them.

YOUR ROADMAP - PROJECT MANAGEMENT MADE EASY

You're asking yourself about now, "Why would I want to create a roadmap? I already know what I want to do. Besides, that's going to require a LOT more time than I have right now."

Here's why you want to take the time to create your roadmap. It will help you:

- ✓ Communicate your project plans at a glance.
- ✓ Create graphics and Gantt charts to help you visualize your progress.
- ✓ Establish a clear, shared understanding of your project plans, especially at the board and executive levels. Everyone on your team needs to know where they are going and how to get there.
- ✓ If you have stakeholders such as investors, they'll need to know what to expect, and when.
- ✓ Set out your timeline so you know when things should get started and when they will be completed.
- ✓ Establish the workstreams that give you the ability to coordinate your team – who and when and what and how.
- ✓ Know the status of key milestones and their due dates so you can complete them on time.
- ✓ Explain where your resources — both financial and human — and budget are being allocated.
- ✓ Clearly explain the status of your project at all times.
- ✓ Master your details.

Keeping Your Roadmap Up-to-Date

Once you've created your beautiful, audacious roadmap, KEEP IT UP-TO-DATE. When timelines change, items shift or are deleted, new iterations have been launched, or your budget is out of whack, update your roadmap so it has the most current information. ***Always.***

Take a look at what this process looks like in a project management Gantt chart in ClickUp[6]:

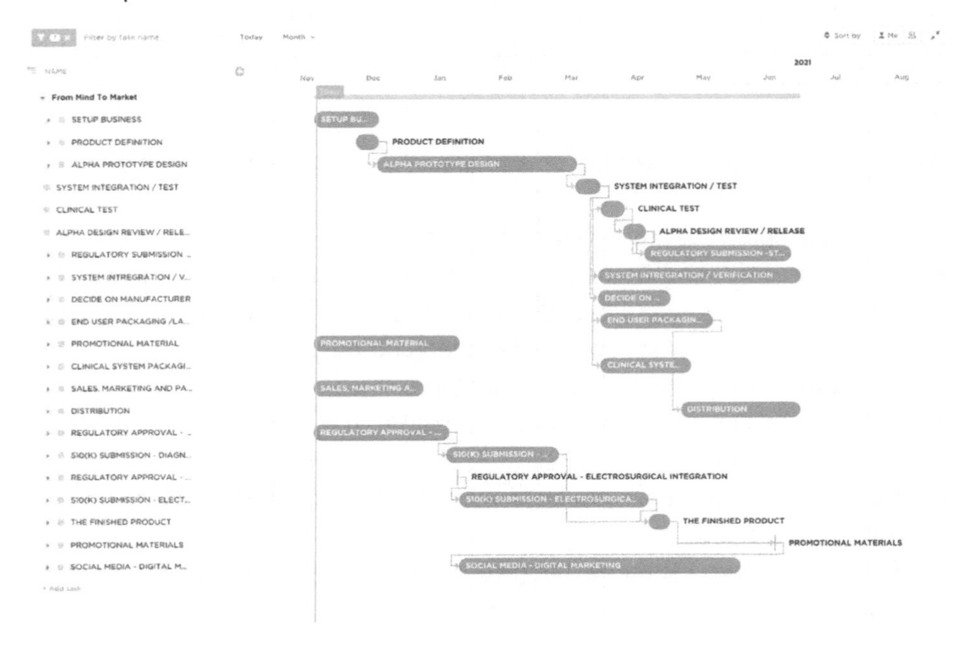

As you can see, the process is linear and sequential. You start by doing the first step, and then the next step, and so on. In some instances, you will be managing several details of the project at the same time, but you can always see what they are, when they are due, and who you need to collaborate with to get things done on time.

Before you know it, and before you pull your hair out (well, maybe just a little hair), you'll reach completion.

You might be surprised how many entrepreneurs, and even seasoned businesspeople, jump ahead or do these steps out of order because of enthusiasm, ignorance, inexperience, arrogance, or plain ol' impatience. Don't. Just don't. There's a reason it works this way: it's because it works this way. Do it sequentially and you'll greatly increase your chances of success. Pinky swear.

Learn how to add a free, ready-to-go Product Launch ClickUp Template here: www.BrainToBank.com/Resources.

Other Great Digital Action Plans

While we love ClickUp for its fantastic action-plan capabilities, it isn't the only resource available to help you build and launch your roadmap to success. Many of the leading roadmap programs on the market are incredibly powerful and comprehensive and can be used by both amateurs and professionals to bring their ideas from brain to bank.

The key is to find the resource that offers the interface and learning curve that best fits your needs and then get started quickly.

However, it can be tempting to pour too much time and effort into building your digital action plan, and you risk losing valuable time and resources by spending too much energy on any one tool. *Please don't lose sight of the reason you are using this tool.*

CHAPTER 2 - Action Accelerators

Take action on these items NOW to keep driving your idea from Brain to Bank:

1. Set up your free ClickUp account here: www.BrainToBank.com/Resources.

2. If you used the ClickUp link above, you should have two templates already uploaded. Choose the classic New Product Development Process or the FDA New Product Development Process template, depending on which your product or service requires.

3. Add your best guestimates to the dates column to complete the timeline and take a look at the Gantt chart view. Isn't it beautiful?

4. Tweak anything you need to change, knowing that as you move ahead in the process of your project you will have more information to better estimate your timeline, milestones, and completion.

5. You can invite others to view your timeline as needed.

6. Know that as you work your way through this book you will define and refine the steps and dates in the timeline. It is an ongoing process.

7. Visit your project often and revel in the line items you have already completed.

Chapter 3

Paving the Road: Your Strategic Plan

NAVIGATING THE JUNGLE

When I was fifteen years old, I traveled to Mexico with my father, who was a world explorer and adventurer. Along with other family members and paying passengers, we rafted the Usumacinta River, which defines part of the border between Guatemala and Mexico.

The Usumacinta was an important trade route for the ancient Mayan civilization and is still for its ancestral tribes, who still live in the region.

As we navigated these remote waters, we spotted live crocodiles, parrots, howler monkeys, and other creatures that made us realize this was the real deal and not Disney's Jungle Cruise.

Mouths gaped. Cameras clicked. We were awestruck.

Part of this adventure trip included a land expedition to Yaxchilan, the spectacular Mayan ruins on the Mexican side of the river. This Mayan city peaked between 681 and 800 A.D., and we were going to explore it in its entirety.

To get to the ruins, we hiked through the dense, humid jungle and used machetes to whack at the limbs and branches that continually blocked the trail. When we finally emerged from the jungle into an overgrown clearing, the ancient ruins looming before us were more than impressive. They were amazing!

We stayed several hours, taking in the majesty and the wonder of how a magnificent city such as this had been built with no construction equipment, just bare hands, brawn, and brute determination.

Even then, I knew my father's ability to find and lead our little expedition to such an extraordinary site was due to his mastery of strategic planning. He had focused on the goal: reach the Yaxchilan Mayan ruins.

He had strategized what it would take to get there, plotted each move, and then flawlessly executed the plan.

A simplified version looks like this:

Strategic Focus	Mayan Ruins Expedition
Mission	Where we are going and why.
Values	Experience and learn about Mayan ancient culture and life.
Vision	Find the ruins and explore.
Goals	Explore Yaxchilan.
Strategies	Take the major route through the jungle.
Implementation	Stop on the river at the mark on the map indicating the jungle route. Hike the route until we reach the destination of the Mayan ruins.

So, you're getting the analogy, right? You're going on an adventure!

Finding a Partner in Your Journey

When I was journeying down the Usumacinta River, I never felt unsafe. I knew no matter what we came up against, we could overcome the obstacles because we had an experienced guide with us who had traveled this river before – my father. I put my trust in him and he never failed me. Because of my father's meticulous planning, we were always able to complete our adventure and arrive at the take-out point safe and on time.

In the same way, entrepreneurs find they need to invest in partners who can help them arrive safely, on schedule, and within budget.

You may fancy yourself as the next Steve Jobs or Mark Zuckerberg, but – *spoiler alert* – both of those trail-blazing innovators had partners who helped them find lucrative footholds and make connections in the industry where their brilliance could thrive.

Wondering how you start the process of finding a partner or mentor? Here are some tips on how to identify and reach out to a potential partner in your pursuit of moving from mind to market:

Step 1: Identify A Potential Partner

There are several ways you can identify a potential partner in your enterprise; the only limitations are your own creativity and confidence. Here are a few ideas to get you down the road to identifying a potential partner:

- Ask around through your network for ideas on who to contact.
- Search the web's resources for finding start-up or product development co-founders.
- Join product-development and start-up groups to source potential partners.
- Attend a start-up accelerator or boot camp to network with potential partners.
- If you have a mentor, ask him/her for names of individuals and groups, and, hopefully, a "warm introduction" to them.

As you get started on your wish list of potential partners, you will want to ensure that any partner is in your unique field, has experience bringing ideas to market successfully, and has a personality that will gel with your leadership.

Step 2: Confidently Contact Your Potential Partner

Once you've identified a potential partner, you need to contact them and ask for their support.

For many entrepreneurs, this is a difficult step to take. Admitting you need help and cold-calling a potential partner or investor can make you feel you are less than the trail-blazing innovator you see in the mirror every morning. But the truth is, we may see our unassured selves that way, but most others do not. So set aside those fearful thoughts, know that others have done this, and so can you. Before you contact your potential partner, take a swig of humility mixed with quiet confidence. A cocktail of both kinds of courage can be just what you need to invite another person into your vision for success.

Don't be dismayed by rejection. The most sought-after partners are approached by many entrepreneurs who are in need. Don't let *real* rejection kill your dreams, and don't let the *fear* of rejection keep you from reaching out for a potential partnership. Just keep going until you succeed. The right partner for you and your project is out there.

Step 3: Offer a True Partnership

Finally, make sure you are offering your potential partner a true collaboration. A quality partner will be excited to jump in and help you bring your idea to life, but they will want to know their time and efforts are going to be appreciated and rewarded in some way.

Make sure you clearly articulate your passion and purpose for bringing this idea to the market and show them how their involvement will benefit them as well. Whether through a joint investment partnership or a positive financial outcome, give your potential collaborator a reason to buddy up with you besides the "good vibes" that come from helping someone in need.

Never forget: this process is an investment in yourself and your idea. Work hard to find the right partner and reach out as many times as necessary to find that person who is going to help give you the resources, confidence, and encouragement to bring your idea from mind to market.

ADVICE FROM INDUSTRY EXPERTS

I have learned to use the genius of others to bring my own projects to market. I continue to collaborate with the best of the best to ensure my end-product is all that I envision and all that the customer expects... or even more.

My colleague and collaborator for fine-tuning strategic planning is Anthony Taylor. Anthony is a thought leader in strategy and leadership. His management consulting firm, SME Strategy, specializes in helping organizations with their strategic planning process. Here are some tips from the master.[7]

Set Your Strategic Focus

What should you focus on as you plan and strategize?

- Seeking alignment with your mission and vision
- Soliciting input and feedback from everyone involved
- Analyzing trends to understand what is going on in your industry and around the world
- Selecting a handful of priorities to work on so you stay on track as you implement and execute
- Communicating your priorities with colleagues/partners so everyone understands where you're going

You can create endless examples of strategic goals, but if they don't align with where you intend to go or with your strategic priorities, then you're going to be wasting your time, energy, and resources. Focus on the goals that will move you forward to realize your mission or vision.

Industry Strategic Partners

A strategic partnership is an agreed-upon collaboration between businesses that have overlapping or complementary but divergent goals. The ability to distinguish between conventional alliances and those that are truly strategic is a skill to be mastered.

On the "partner beware" side, nobody wants to collaborate with a parasite who sucks time, energy, and resources. Be sure your prospective partners have something to offer you. Just as important, be sure *you* have something to offer and contribute to them, so the benefit is mutual.

A collaboration should be symbiotic, in the sense that both parties, in combining efforts, resources, and information, help each other get an edge in the marketplace. This can include training each other's employees to develop and sell the product or service.

The alliance between Spotify and Uber is an example of a strategic partnership between two companies. Their collaboration has helped both companies increase their customer base: Uber riders enjoy the ability to take control of the stereo and select the music they like, and in doing so they become familiar with what Spotify has to offer. Another example of a strategic partnership would be a medical device company forming alliances with its parts suppliers.

Some of the many benefits of strategic partnerships include:

- Increased revenue
- Expanded customer base
- Expanded geographic reach
- Extended product lines
- Shared resources
- Access to new technologies and IP

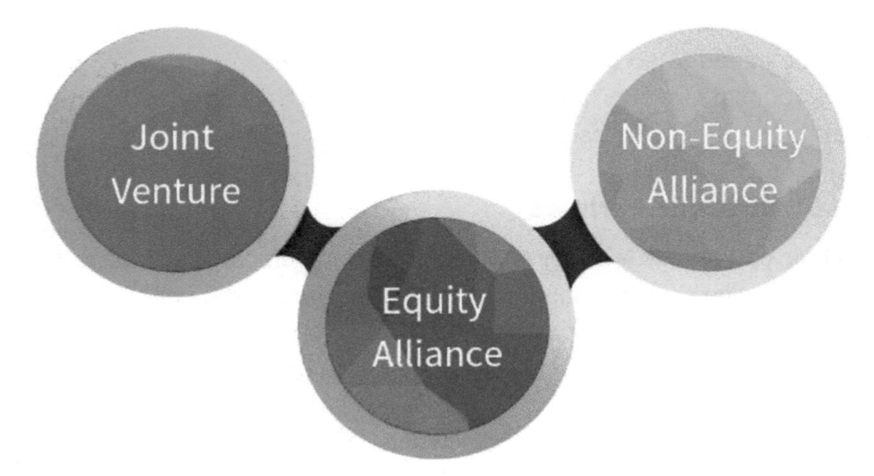

Strategic alliances may be one of these common types:

Equity Strategic Alliance

An equity strategic partnership is when one company purchases equity in another business, also known as a partial acquisition, or when each business purchases equity in the other, also known as a cross-equity transaction.

An example of an equity strategic alliance is Panasonic's $30 million investment in Tesla in the electric-vehicle market and expansion of its drive into green energy businesses.

Non-Equity Strategic Alliance

In this type of alliance, businesses agree to share resources but do not create a separate entity, nor do they share equity. More informal than equity alliances, these arrangements make up the majority of business alliances.

Starbucks is a master at creating non-equity strategic alliances. For example, Barnes and Noble agrees to work with Starbucks by selling Starbucks products in the cafes at B&N. However, B&N does not participate in any of the member benefit programs or the pre-determined standard refill policies at Starbucks' corporate stores. B&N wants to provide more value to their customers by offering premium coffee products, while Starbucks benefits by expanding into new markets at a lower cost. It's a win-win with little paperwork and no equity loss.

Joint Venture

A binding agreement is used to create a Joint Venture (JV), with sharing resources and equity at its core. Profits are split between the two companies, although not necessarily 50/50. An example of a joint venture is drugmaker GlaxoSmithKline's JV with Google parent company Alphabet's start-up Verily Life Sciences to build devices and further research in the developing field of bioelectronics.

Each of these strategic alliances is created for certain needs at specific times in your business cycle. Selecting the right type can mean success for your project.

According to *Ivey Business Journal*[8] there are five criteria of a strategic alliance. An alliance that meets any one of these criteria is strategic and should be managed accordingly:

- Critical to the success of a core business goal or objective
- Critical to the development or maintenance of a core competency or other source of competitive advantage
- Blocks a competitive threat
- Creates or maintains strategic choices for the firm
- Mitigates a significant risk to the business

If any of these five crucial elements exist in the partnership, both organizations benefit from a synergetic relationship that drives and accelerates the business, mitigates competition and threats, and creates a viable presence in the marketplace.

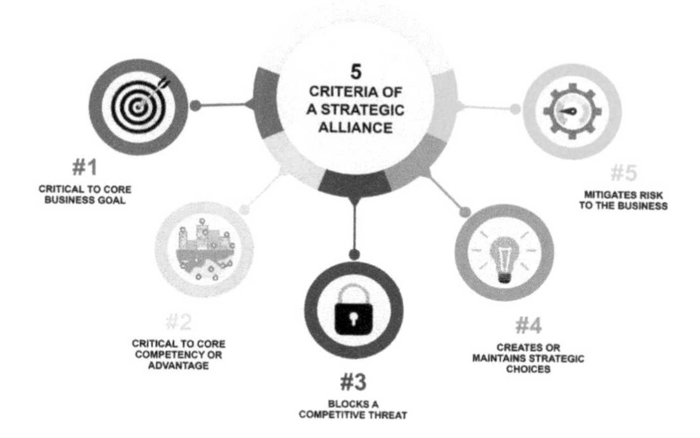

Businesses that do not actively build and maintain strategic partnerships will struggle to create and maintain a competitive edge in a growing, global market.

It's important to realize that strong strategic partnerships require efficient management. It is imperative to choose the correct partner; each project requires comprehensive insight into the partner's sales, marketing, and project data, as well as an understanding of its customers, culture, and company vision.

By correctly utilizing strategic partners, companies can take advantage of additional resources, knowledge, technology, and other sharable resources that would be impossible to access in a solo venture.

Yes, there is safety in numbers.

CHAPTER 3 - Action Accelerators

THINK IT ⟶ ORGANIZE IT ⟶ DO IT

Take action on these items NOW to keep driving your idea from Brain to Bank:

I advise my clients to use Anthony Taylor's Strategic Planning template to complete their strategic plan. This template will guide you through each specific step in the planning process, allowing you to create a focused and actionable plan from scratch that aligns with your specific product or service.

Completing these Roadmap activities will help you identify:

- A common vision of your ideal future as an entrepreneur
- A mission your entire team can get behind
- Your current state, using a SWOT analysis
- Trends affecting your organization
- Measurable goals that will keep you and your team accountable
- Potential risks and roadblocks
- Values and behaviors to be modeled
- An action plan with specific steps and tactics

Start here:

1. Download the Strategic Plan Workbook here: www.BrainToBank.com/Resources.

2. Take the time to complete your Strategic Plan. Today. A lot of this plan will end up in your Business Plan, so be accurate and thorough. One of the many benefits of this exercise is that it forces you to think about the various aspects of your idea, your business, and the actions you need to take to become clear and focused on your goals and get from here to there. If you feel this is an overwhelming task, I suggest taking a Strategic Planning Workshop.

   You can check out suggestions here: www.BrainToBank.com/Resources.

3. What are the goals of your business?

    ____

4. What are the types of companies able to help you achieve those goals? How will you make sure they truly align with your company goals?

    ____

5. What benefits would those potential strategic partners gain by collaborating with you?

    ____

6. Which type of strategic partnership would be best?

    ____

7. What do you have to offer and why you would be a great strategic partner? How will you figure out your potential partner's needs, so you can align your benefits with theirs?

    ____

8. Now go find those companies and build a relationship. When your product is ready, go and provide the value you've been promising.

9. Update your roadmap so it has the most current information.

STICK TO THE PLAN

Chapter 4

Corps, Orgs, & Naming Your Baby

CREATING YOUR BUSINESS ENTITY

What business name and what type of business entity will you select for your project?

Creating a new product or service also means you are creating a business. Whether you are at the stage of licensing your invention, outright selling your idea after it is up and running and making beaucoup bucks or working the business yourself because you love the challenge and thrill of being "in the battlefield" and savor the taste of Tums, you will need a bona fide business name and entity.

Choosing the correct type of entity will do several things for your business:

- Create an official appearance. Corporations have more clout than some other types of entities (such as sole proprietor), and this may make it easier to do business with other companies. For example, strategic partners.
- Give you the edge to attract upscale employees. No employee signs up to work for a fly-by-night company which may be gone tomorrow as soon as the sun rises. Being a legit corporation or LLC will help you feel you can do this... you are doing this... and you will continue to do this successfully. This will attract the right employees for your business. Those employees will catch this contagious "can do" attitude and pass it on to new employees as they come in.
- Help you raise the needed funds by attracting investors, who usually prefer corporations and equity positions. Looking like the real deal is the first step toward getting noticed.

Entity options may include a Limited Liability Corporation (LLC), S Corporation, or C Corporation. The chart below summarizes the different options for an entity:

U.S. Business Entities Comparison Chart

ENTITY TYPE	FORMATION	LIABILITY	TAXATION
Sole Proprietorship (SP)	Easy and inexpensive to create. No filing is necessary.	The owner is personally liable for business debts.	Profit or loss is reported by the owner on his/her personal tax return.
General Partnership (GP)	Easy and inexpensive to create. No filing is necessary.	Partners assume unlimited joint and several personal liabilities for business debts.	Profit or loss is reported by each partner (owner) on his/her tax return.
Limited Partnership (LP)	Mostly used for companies investing in real estate. More expensive to form than GP.	If limited partners do not participate in management, then they have limited personal liability for business debts up to the amount of their investment.	Similar to a dividend, each partner receives a return on their investment as defined in the partnership agreement.
Limited Liability Company (LLC)	More expensive to establish than a partnership or sole proprietorship.	Offers limited liability protection and pass-through taxation. Owners are usually not personally responsible for the business debts and liabilities.	An LLC is usually treated as a pass-through entity for federal income tax purposes. The LLC itself pays taxes on business income. The members of the LLC pay personal taxes on their share of the LLC's profits.
C-Corp	More expensive to establish than a partnership or sole proprietorship. A C-Corp can have an unlimited number of shareholders.	Owners have personal liability for business debts.	The profit of a corporation is taxed to the corporation when earned and then is taxed to the shareholders when distributed as dividends = double tax. Shareholders cannot deduct any loss of the corporation.
S-Corp	More expensive to establish than a partnership or sole proprietorship. The number of shareholders is limited to 100.	Owners are not personally responsible for the business debts and liabilities.	Income is apportioned to owners according to ownership interests. Owners report their share of corporate profit or loss on their tax returns and can offset income from other sources by utilizing corporate loss.
Professional Corporation (PC)	More expensive to establish than a partnership or sole proprietorship. All owners must belong to the same profession.	Owners have liability for their own acts of malpractice, but no personal liability for other owners.	PCs have the same taxation benefits as a corporation.
Non-Profit Corporation (NPO)	Common types of nonprofits include 501(c)(3), 501(c)(4) & 501(c)(7) organizations. Each type has certain benefits and restrictions.	A non-profit corporation is formed to carry out a charitable, educational, religious, or literary purpose.	Only qualified groups formed for charitable, literary, educational, or scientific purposes receive full tax advantages. Business expenses can be deducted.

If you are incorporating in a country other than the U.S., be sure to check local entity formation requirements.

NOTE: *As always with something this important and involving the law, consult an attorney or CPA to select the correct entity for your tax implications and state requirements.*

Where should I create my entity? My home state? Delaware? Nevada?

For the most part, venture capital firms and angel investors prefer Delaware corporations. To avoid added costs and complexities, most small businesses choose to incorporate in their home state.

Again, consult an attorney or CPA to select the correct entity for your tax situation and state requirements.

Another Episode in the Entrepreneur Drama Series
I Didn't See It Coming

I worked with a new start-up that imported products used in high-adventure, extreme-adrenaline sports and in explorations. The founders had heard Delaware and Nevada offered anonymity to corporations and their officers/members. They also thought it was hip and sexy to incorporate in a cool state like Nevada, as "everyone else is doing it". Nevada's tax laws would be an advantage when they hit it big, so why not start looking prestigious and important from the get-go?

They went online and found a company with step-by-step instructions on how to set up a corporation in Nevada. It came complete with a Nevada address, Registered Nevada Agent, and Nevada business license.

Here's where the lessons began: after the initial paperwork...which was like getting a colonoscopy without anesthesia... they finally got their incorporation documents and state business license.

What they didn't anticipate was the jacked-up cost of maintaining that out-of-state corporation, license, and Registered Agent after the first year. The ongoing costs were more expensive than incorporating in their own state. A lot more.

They had not done their homework. They had made things more difficult, more time-consuming, and more expensive by not investigating all of the alternatives first.

In the end, I got them out of Nevada and incorporated in their home state, which was much cheaper and easier for their struggling start-up.

So, do this instead: Make sure the benefit of an out-of-your-state business entity is really what you need and you're willing to shell out the extra money to maintain it. Otherwise, it's home sweet home.

WEBSITES AND DOMAINS AND URLS

Fear of the dot-com and having to figure out how to choose a name for a website is a common malady among new entrepreneurs. Often questions such as *Where do I find a domain name? How much will it cost? Do I have to have a dot-com, or can I choose another extension?* and *What if the name I want is already taken?* induce indecision paralysis and can stop you from moving ahead. So do the simplest step first: research a name until you have your URL.

Because a website and domain name are usually essential to conducting and sustaining a business, it's important to choose them wisely. Availability for your business name and URL (i.e., your domain name and your address as a World Wide Web page) often dictate what you'll end up with.

I am constantly surprised at how many domain names are not available because someone else already owns them. Type any normal name you can think of, and many not-so-normal names, into GoDaddy.com and you will see this message: Domain Taken.

Seriously? Somebody already thought up my awesome, unique name? And then they bought it? And a website is not even up with that name? They're just "holding it"? Rats!

When I typed in GoDogGo.com for a new Uber business for pets I got "Domain Taken." But then there were dozens of alternative suggestions:

- godoggone.com
- gopoochgo.com
- gohoundgo.com
- movedogmove.com
- walkdogwalk.com
- runpoochrun.com
- movepoochmove.com
- movecaninemove.com
- gomuttgo.net
- runmuttrun.com
- movemuttmove.com
- runcaninerun.com
- gocaninego.net
- gopoochgo.net
- gohoundgo.net
- movehoundmove.com
- gocaninego.org
- gomuttgo.org
- gomuttgo.pet
- godoggo.guru

GoPoochGo.com somehow didn't have the same ring. Neither did GoMuttGo.com. But GoDogGo.guru... now maybe I could really knock that one out of the park with the right marketing. Hmmmmmmm.

The point is, don't get too stuck on a name you can't get. Besides, if you choose one too closely related to a website selling a similar product or service, chances are when people google your business the other company will show up first in the search and get the click. You lose.

Get creative. Some of the best-known names are completely made up: Häagen-Dazs, Vitol, Accenture, Xerox, Hydrock, Kodak, Pantone, Sony, Google, IKEA.

A word of caution: unless you have money to burn (I checked... MoneyToBurn.com is taken... I know, it's a hot name), stay away from the premium domain names that will cost you thousands of dollars. You're not so big and important that you have to flush money on one of these expensive URLs. Instead, get creative and figure out something that explains your product and also attracts inquisitive customers.

Think like you own the alphabet. Check GoDaddy.com to see if you can get a domain name that includes your business name "inside" an available domain name. For example: www.GoDogGo.com becomes www.GoDogGoRides.com.

And by all means, have fun with this. Besides your dog, cat, and kids, how many things do you actually get to name?

The Value of Brand Management

Brand Management: It's Not Just for Celebrities Anymore

In today's world of digital-first marketing and consumer behavior, it's more important than ever that you have a digital brand identity. What does a brand entail?

- Print Media
- Video Advertising
- Social Media Management
- Online Platform Management
- Content Curation
- Branding Best Practices
- Logos & Graphics

I know, it's enough to make your head spin. The importance of brand management — especially in the digital space — is why so many companies have invested huge amounts of human resource dollars into hiring top-tier social media and digital marketing managers. Some businesses hire full agencies on retainer just to manage their online identity — and avoid potential digital disaster. If you are beginning to bring your idea from brain to bank, you're probably not quite ready to hire a digital agency to manage your online presence. However, there are some simple steps you can take while you are in the business set-up stage to boost that digital presence.

5 Steps to a Fool-Proof Digital Brand

1. Develop Your Brand

Does your LLC or product have a brand identity? If you haven't thought through the colors, names, imagery, and voice of your brand, now is the time to invest in building out your company identity.

Whether you partner with a graphic designer to give you potential ideas to pick from, or you create designs on your own, make sure you select a brand identity that fits your product as well as your business at large. This brand will be traveling with you for a long time, and the less you have to renovate it, the better.

2. Set Up Your Brand Best Practices

While you are likely the main (or only) individual in charge of your communications, soon you will want to bring on other individuals who can manage these time-intensive resources for you. To help them protect your brand's identity, it can be beneficial to create a brand best practices document.

This document can be a work in progress as you grow and scale, but here are some top aspects to include:

- Your Name, Product Names, and Key Leadership
- Fonts, Graphics, and Logos
- A Description of Your "Voice"
- Target Audience and Key Demographics
- Competitor Brands
- Your Minimum Viable Product (MVP)
- Your 30-Second Elevator Pitch

Creating a best practices document can be a huge help to anyone with whom you may partner to build and develop your brand online or in print.

3. Create & Optimize Your Website

Would you believe that websites are still the main way consumers and investors learn about your brand and product? It's true. Visiting your website will be the primary way consumers interact with your brand online. The better your website is, the more likely they will make a purchasing decision.

If you haven't created a website for your idea, it's time to start thinking about how you will build one that showcases your future product or business in the best way. You may also want to look up Search Engine Optimization (SEO) to start learning how to best help your brand show up on Google and other search engines.

4. Create Accounts Where It Counts

Once you have a handle on your brand and website, you will want to create some social media accounts for your business.

The world of social media has exploded over the past few years, and knowing which platform is right for your idea is essential. You may be tempted to create an account on every single platform, but if you aren't ready to hire a full-time social media manager, it may be best to focus on the accounts that best connect to your key demographic and audience.

5. Think Through Digital Advertising

You may not be ready quite yet to invest in digital marketing and advertising, but it never hurts to start thinking about how you will engage with online sales. There are plenty of online resources you can use to learn more about how to set up and run effective digital ads that will drive traffic to your website and other online channels. Start reading up on how these systems work and learn how to invest in them when the time comes.

CHAPTER 4 - Action Accelerators

Take action on these items NOW to keep driving your idea from Brain to Bank:

1. Talk with an attorney and CPA to determine which business entity type is best for you. Both legal and tax advice will help you decide which entity type ... and which location for it... will serve you best.

2. Decide on a name for your new business:

   - Check your state corporation site to determine if the name is available.
   - Check GoDaddy or other domain-selling companies to see if the URL is available. If the exact name is already taken (most are), try variations of that name until you find one that works for you. Buy it.
   - Reserve the name for your corporation.

3. Either hire someone to complete your corporation registration, operating agreement, and business license, or do it yourself.

   Hiring one-stop online shops is great for getting all the needed paperwork completed. They can assist with a range of required documents and you won't have the frustration of having to "learn the ropes" on filling them out or of parsing all the "legalese." Just remember, you get what you pay for.

4. Create a brand best practices document. Here are things to include:

   - Your Name, Product Names, and Key Leadership
   - Fonts, Graphics, and Logos
   - A Description of Your "Voice"
   - Target Audience & Key Demographics
   - Competitor Brands
   - Your Minimum Viable Product (MVP)
   - Your 30-Second Elevator Pitch

Creating a best practices document can be a huge help to anyone with whom you partner to build and develop your brand online or in print.

5. Update your roadmap so it has the most current information.

STICK TO THE PLAN

Chapter 5

Writing Your Business Plan

THE MOTHER ROAD

I'm a fairly good driver. The fact that I can double-clutch a Porsche Carrera 4 rounding a corner at 100 miles an hour has gotten me a date or two with like-minded, fast drivers who sport tight-fitting jumpsuits and milk mustaches. When I'm on the track, I'm driving around and around on an oval-shaped road, so I don't have to know where I am going. I just go.

Truth be known, I have orientational dyslexia. If I am supposed to go right, I will go left because that's what I think I am supposed to do. I seldom know if I am going north or south, or east or west, unless the sun is directly in my eyes or behind me. So, I tell the nice people who so kindly (and often) give me directions to not use the four compass coordinates but tell me right or left at specific landmarks. And then I go the wrong way anyway. I have found myself stranded in more than one cow pasture in the middle of nowhere. Moooooove.

Over time, I have learned to simply leave early so I have time to get lost. If a miracle occurs and I arrive without some circuitous detours interfering, then I sit in my car and do some work or read a book that I brought along, just in case. Now, although I use a digital map on my phone with the voice of my Australian sexy man "Simon" guiding my journey, I also take a printed map with me as a backup plan. It's not always a simple matter of, "Simon says this, Simon says that."

When I am driving long distances, such as on the Mother Road from L.A. to Chicago, I'm fastidious about using a very detailed map to get me from here to there. You can't always trust the GPS. I also know there are a kazillion stops I could make along the way to explore old Route 66 stuff, but which ones are the most important to me? What do I really want to see? I'll need to plan my side trips, too. Otherwise, I'll get lost and waste a lot of valuable time. Plus, I may never get to my final destination.

Same for your business. You wouldn't drive Route 66's 2,448 miles without a map, so don't start your business without writing your business plan; it's your roadmap to success.

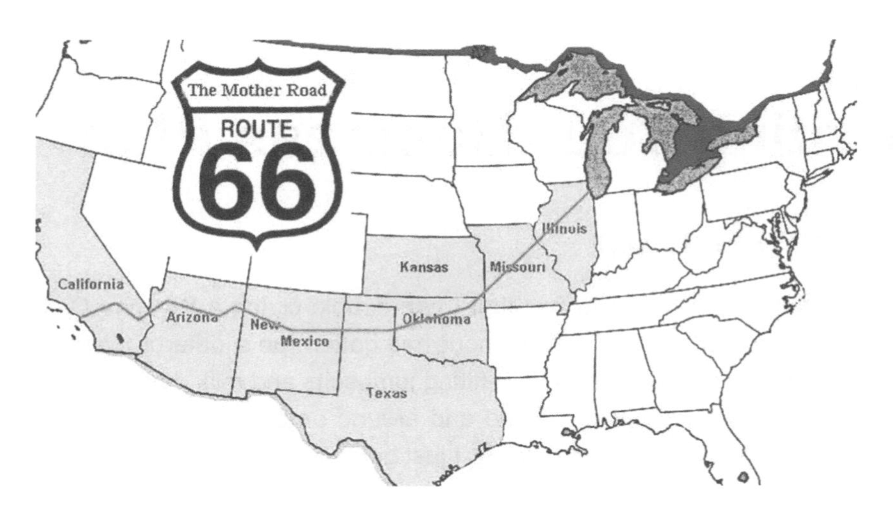

Another Episode in the Entrepreneur Drama Series
I Didn't See It Coming

A few years ago, I was involved in an M&A (Mergers & Acquisitions) transaction for a consumer products company that had decided to partner with a much larger corporation to reap the many benefits of a strategic partner.

We were knee-deep in due diligence (the buyer's/investor's investigation of the company) and working frantically to provide all of the requested and required documents to the big corp:

1. Company Business Plan
    a. Company Historical Background Information
    b. Industry Overview
    c. Competitors — Comparative Strengths and Weaknesses
    d. Product Descriptions
    e. Product Development Plans
    f. Sales and Marketing Plans
    g. Operational, Headcount, and Capital Expenditures Budgets
    h. Pro Forma Financial Plan
2. Company Organizational Documents, Articles of Incorporation, Operating Agreement, Certificate of Good Standing, Corporate Charter, Board of Directors Meeting Minutes, including Committee Minutes

3. Historical State and Federal Tax Returns
4. Ownership Ledger
5. Business Insurance Policies and Summary
6. Litigation — Past, Existing, and Threatened
7. Material Contracts
8. Facilities Lease Agreements
9. Equipment Lease Agreements
10. Employee Handbook
11. Employee Roster and Payroll Data
12. Benefits Plans
13. Customer List and Contact Information
14. Supplier List and Contact Information
15. Accounts Receivables Aging
16. Accounts Payable Aging
17. Historical Property, Plant, and Equipment, and Depreciation Records
    a. Last Five Years
    b. Historical Monthly, Quarterly, and Annual Financial Statements
18. Annual CPA Audits and/or Compilation Reports (Last Five Years)
19. Management and Board of Directors Bios and CVs
20. Last Year's Operational, Headcount, and Capital Expenditures
    a. Budgets
21. Current Year Operational, Headcount, and Capital Expenditures
    a. Budgets
22. Key Contact Information:
    a. Attorneys
    b. CPAs
    c. Commercial Banks
    d. Insurance Broker
    e. Outside Board Members
    f. Outside Advisors
23. Risk Factors
24. Investor PowerPoint Presentation

Where do you suppose the company I consulted with got stuck in providing the required documents? Ummmmmm... the title of this chapter?

Right on. They had never written a business plan for a business they had been running for over a decade.

Who does that? You'd be surprised.

Not having thought through their business to the degree that a business plan forces you to think, and not then writing it down and following it, was the reason they had wandered off course and now needed an investor partner rescue. We had to write the business plan retroactively. They still needed one.

You figured out the lesson learned here, correct? Don't start down the road blindly following the voice of Simon Says on your GPS without a well-thought-out roadmap. Yes, it takes time now, but later you will avoid costly, even disastrous, mistakes. Doing it right today will increase the value of your company tomorrow. Write your business plan. Then run your company like it's for sale every day.

WHAT'S YOUR STORY?

People connect to stories. After attending a presentation or reading stuff on your website or listening to your podcast, people don't remember the joke you told at the beginning, the horrific statistics and numbers you quoted, or the pain points you elaborated upon. They remember your story. What's your story? Your story should include the following attributes:

- What's the problem in the marketplace? How did it affect you?
- What solution does your business offer? How did the solution help start your business?
- What's the go-to-market strategy? What did this do for your business?
- How does your solution make money (i.e., implementation)? How did this help your company make money?
- How is your solution different from the competition's? Why does it work?
- How do you grow the business?

Storytelling connects us to others and helps us understand the world we live in. Stories communicate our values and beliefs and help us identify with one another.

Compelling stories tap into our emotions strongly, authentically connecting us and helping us believe in a business and what it stands for.

Storytelling conveys purpose, and businesses with purpose are the ones that ultimately stand out and capture consumers' hearts and wallets.

CHOOSING THE RIGHT FORMAT

The real value of creating a business plan lies not in having a completed plan you can pass out on demand, but rather in the process of researching and thinking about your business in an organized, methodical manner. Working your way through your business plan helps you to think things through thoroughly and critically analyze your idea and how you will get it from brain to bank.

For whom should you write your business plan?

- Founders
- Investors
- Employees
- Customers
- Future Owners

There are several ways to write a business plan encompassing your various audiences. The important thing is to ensure that your plan describes your project in detail and puts you through the much-needed exercise of getting your idea out of your head and into a doable, action-packed roadmap.

Traditional

The most common business plan format has been around a long time and requires more work than the newer, sleeker models. This format is longer in nature but includes a lot of information that ultimately forces you to think through your idea/ business in great detail. This can be a good thing, as many entrepreneurs and inventors can't wait to get into the thick of it and dive right in with the creation process without thinking things through.

The traditional format is very specific and comprehensive. Here are the sections in a typical business plan:

I. Executive Summary
II. General Company Description
III. Products and Services
IV. Marketing Plan
V. Operational Plan
VI. Management and Organization

VII. Personal Financial Statement
VIII. Start-up Expenses and Capitalization
IX. Financial Plan
X. Appendices

You can work through the sections in any order you like, except for the Executive Summary, which should be done last. It typically takes several weeks to complete a good, traditional business plan. Most of that time is spent in research and in rethinking your ideas and assumptions. But then, that's the value of the process, isn't it?

For a complete checklist to help you write your complete business plan, go here: www.BrainToBank.com/Resources.

ADVICE FROM INDUSTRY EXPERTS

The good news is this: things have progressed rapidly and have been simplified by newcomers in the online business plan market. I have researched and used many, and my fave is LivePlan, created by Palo Alto Software.[9]

LivePlan makes creating your business plan very simple. You get a step-by-step process to follow — they ask you questions and you plug in the answers. They have real sample business plans to help you and it's all online, which means editing and enhancing your business plan as you move ahead is just that much easier.

For financials, LivePlan tells you exactly what kind of financial information you need to enter, and then it does all the calculations automatically using built-in formulas. So you end up with razor-accurate financial statements that include all the tables a lender or investor expects to see.
Once your plan is done, you can:

- Customize the look of your plan using 10 beautiful document themes
- Download your plan as a PDF or Word doc so you can share it easily
- Print out your plan to get a clean, professional document

This is what their long version consists of:
- Executive Summary
    - Opportunity
    - Expectations

- Opportunity
    - Problem & Solution
    - Target Market
    - Competition
- Execution
    - Marketing & Sales
    - Operations
    - Milestones & Metrics
- Company
    - Overview
    - Team
- Financial Plan
    - Forecast
    - Financing
    - Statements
- Appendix
    - Profit and Loss Statement
    - Balance Sheet
    - Cash Flow Statement

One-Pager

With a high-level focus and less time needed to write, this lean start-up business plan is becoming more popular. Concentrating on summarizing the most important points of the key elements of your plan allows you to complete the task much quicker.

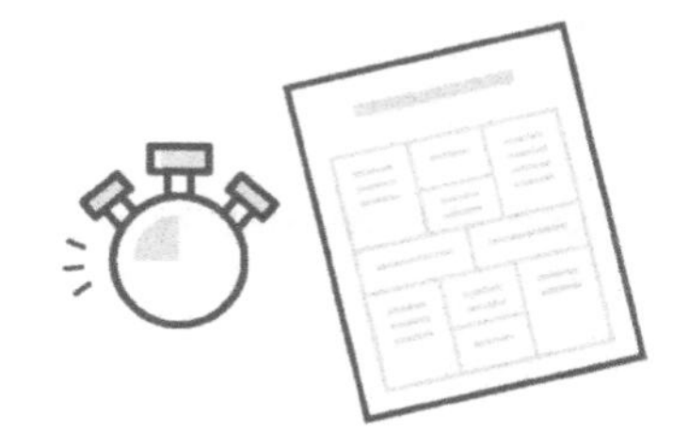

You should know going in that although the one-pager is a great bird's-eye visual, if investors are truly interested in your project, they will ask for more details... a lot more. So don't think this time-saving format will mean you don't have to write the more traditional version.

At some point, you'll need to detail essential sections such as the demographics and avatar (a customer avatar — sometimes referred to as a buyer persona, marketing persona, or customer profile — is a representation of your ideal customer, the type of person you want to purchase your products or services) of your target market, create compelling marketing strategies, and generate the needed financials to give yourself and your investors the confidence to move ahead.

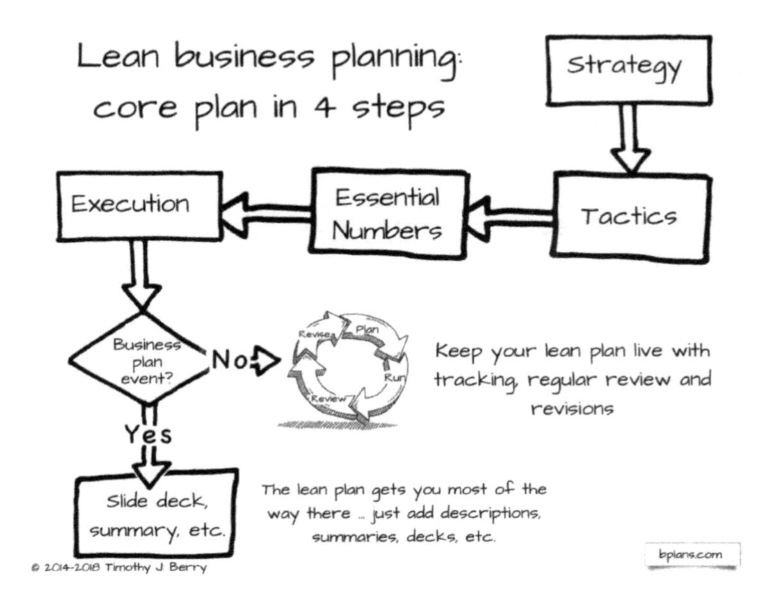

In the end, there's nothing like the thrill of seeing your plan on paper... even one sheet of paper.[10] It's a great place to jump-start your initial business plan.

Once you have mastered your one-sheet, you can expand from there, as the core concepts will already be in place: [11]

Executive Summary
Opportunity
Expectations

Opportunity
Problem & Solution
Target Market
Competition

Execution
Marketing & Sales
Operations
Milestones & Metrics

Company
Overview
Team

Financial Plan
Forecast
Financing
Statements

Appendix

It's as easy as painting by the numbers.

Is your paintbrush ready?

Hold Your Horses: What Is an MVP?

At some point in your business plan development process, you will need to declare what your MVP is.
No, your MVP is not YOU.

In the product development world, an MVP is a minimum viable product. Knowing what your MVP is can be a fast and effective way to communicate both your product as well as your future expectations for the product once it is brought to life on the market.

If you are unable to explain your MVP, potential partners, investors, and even consumers may struggle to connect with your idea and be unwilling to make a purchasing decision.

Driving your business without an MVP is like putting diesel fuel into your smart car for a road trip.

- Is the diesel — whatever you have instead of an MVP— *technically* fuel? Yes.
- Will you run into all sorts of problems once you head down the road? Most likely.
- Will the tow truck operator think you are crazy when you tell him why your car is smoking on the side of the road? Definitely.

As you build your business plan, make sure you have identified (and can communicate) that your minimum viable product is essential to your success.

An MVP is essential because it is the key means of validating an idea or product at its earliest stage of development. Though the product itself may not technically exist yet, the MVP should be clearly defined and easy to communicate.

Take software products, for example. Knowing the MVP can help early beta testers give helpful feedback to you and your development team as they seek to use the product. If the software isn't operating as it should or producing the right results according to your MVP, then there is a tangible item that you can review and update, fix, or delete.

MVPs are built on lean and agile methodology. This means validation and iteration are key to ensuring the final outcome is successful with the least amount of production friction involved.

WHY DO I NEED TO DEFINE MY MVP?

Many entrepreneurs see defining an MVP as a laborious process that can simply be skipped in favor of more lucrative steps.

However, skipping over the defining and development of an MVP can cause you to fly down the road without knowing how to operate your windshield wipers. Sure, if there's no rain you may be okay. But the moment that storm hits, you're in trouble.

Once you get to the point of product development with your idea, your MVP is going to pay huge dividends toward your success. Once you bring in a product team to help put muscles and flesh on the bones of your idea, your MVP will help:

- Bring your potential product to the market with as few obstacles or hiccups as possible.
- Offer a real-world testing environment where you can get invaluable feedback from those who may be paying money for your product someday.
- Analyze and optimize your target market, audience, and demographics earlier in the process.

Defining your MVP is a key step in your business plan, as it shows potential investors and future employees that you have put the time and effort into making sure your idea has legs in today's market. Being able to communicate your MVP will help you from this point forward.

CHAPTER 5 - Action Accelerators

Take action on these items NOW to keep driving your idea from Brain to Bank:

1. Conduct research and locate all of the necessary information you will need to complete your business plan. Use the SBA Checklist in: www.BrainToBank.com/Resources.

2. Compile information on your Minimum Viable Product (MVP).

3. Complete an online one-page Pitch Plan here: www.BrainToBank.com/Resources.

4. LivePlan does not have a free trial, but it does come with a 60-day money-back guarantee. This means you do pay when you sign up, but you have two months to figure out whether it's right for you. If it's not, you can request a full refund and they will honor it, no questions asked. You have NO reason to wait... get started NOW!

5. Now complete the longer LivePlan version.

6. Update your roadmap so it has the most current information.

STICK TO THE PLAN

Chapter 6

Financials, Budgets, and Valium

UNDERSTANDING BUSINESS FINANCIALS

For those of us who prefer pictures and words to numbers, understanding business financials is as daunting a task as climbing Mount Everest is to those who hate to be cold. We are not equipped to climb icy slopes, the frigid air is making our heads hurt, and Valium can't calm us down because it produces mind-altering effects at a time when preservation of mental competence is extremely critical. So now what?

Baby steps. You take tiny, dig-your-ice-cleats-into-the-mountain baby steps. For sure it will be challenging, but you won't likely slip or fall, and you'll eventually get where you want to go.

I once had the insane notion that I wanted to become an investment banker. I knew from previous experience my attempts at learning financial equations and formulas were like teaching a fish to ride a bicycle.

© Artwork Ray Troll 1993

Then I thought: I have already been in the Mergers & Acquisitions (M&A) field for a decade, preparing the operations side of a business for sale by building effective business infrastructures and identifying, creating, and implementing growth opportunities. So how hard could learning financial stuff be?

I desperately wanted to acquire this much-needed skill and was determined conquer it. So, I signed up for an online course for an Investment Banking Series 79 license.[12]

Over the next year, I studied for more than 200 hours for the exam. To my crushing disappointment, I missed passing it by 2 percent.

Being the determined person I am, I doggedly studied for another 200 hours and took the exam again. I missed passing it by one question. One question!

About now I should have given up and realized that the left side of my brain was either atrophied or nonexistent. But I didn't give up. I didn't tell myself I'll never understand this part of business. I got busy figuring out how to get to the top of that mountain. So...

I studied for another 200 hours. Finally! I passed the exam! Woohooo!

The point is this: for some people, numbers, math, and business financials come easily. If you're in the not-so-great-at-numbers group, you're certainly not alone (I can see you counting others...see, you do know how to do numbers :-). But to run a successful business, you will need the basics, and you can — with less effort than 200 x 3 hours — learn what you need to successfully guide your company in a well-informed, financially savvy manner.

The Basics: Breaking It Down Without Having a Breakdown

Being able to track the financials of your company affects many areas of your business. For starters:

- Setting up your budget
- Creating pro formas
- Tracking cash flow
- Managing financials
- Risk management
- Breakeven points

- Burn rate[13]
- Cost of Goods Sold (COGS)
- Pricing structure
- Setting up a payment system
- Merchant accounts
- Relationships with banks
- Loans
- Investors
- Grants
- Taxes

Because most start-ups experience losses and negative cash flow in the beginning, it's imperative to keep an eye on your money so there's enough cash on hand to pay employees, vendors, and suppliers. Planning and budgeting for these and other financial necessities is critical to keeping money efficiently moving through.

As you grow into a larger organization, you will be measuring Key Performance Indicators (KPIs) and producing the various types of reports needed by management, shareholders, and investors. This requires a comprehensive financial management system that can gauge the profitability of the company and its investments.

You don't have to be a "numbers person." But you do want to develop the financial acumen necessary to interpret financial reports and make decisions based on available data, manage inventory and receivables, create an accurate budget, and run COGS in a product or service.

Plus, understanding your income taxes can keep the IRS hounds from howling on your doorstep.

Financial reports contain an enormous amount of information about your company's past, present, and future. When you can understand and analyze the three key essential reports — income, balance, and cash flow — you'll gain valuable insights into your company's strengths and weaknesses. You can also detect trends — good and not-so-good — so you can keep going down that road or course-correct if needed.

ADVICE FROM INDUSTRY EXPERTS

Corporate Finance Institute (CFI) is the leading provider of online financial analyst certification programs. Even if you have no intention of becoming an analyst (and most of us don't), there is much to be learned that will help you understand the numbers of your business and make better financial decisions. The following is a short, yet essential, overview from CFI of basic financials you should understand.[14]

Overview of the Three Financial Statements

Being able to read and understand financial statements is a much-needed skill if you are to comprehend your company's financial health. By mastering this part of your business, you'll be able to make informed decisions and improve your Return on Investment (ROI).

The three key financial statements are: (1) the Income Statement, (2) the Balance Sheet, and (3) the Cash Flow Statement. These three core reports are intricately linked to each other, and you will at the very least need to understand each of them.

Income Statement

Often, the first thing an investor or analyst will look at is the income statement. The income statement shows the performance of the business throughout each period, displaying sales revenue at the very top. The statement then deducts the Cost of Goods Sold (COGS) to find gross profit. From there, the gross profit is adjusted to account for other operating expenses and income, depending on the nature of the business, to reach net income at the bottom — "the bottom line" — for the business.

Key features:

- Shows the revenues and expenses of a business
- Expressed over a period of time (i.e., 1 year, 1 quarter, Year-to-Date, etc.)
- Uses accounting principles such as matching and accruals to represent figures (not presented on a cash basis)
- Used to assess profitability

Balance Sheet

The balance sheet displays the company's assets, liabilities, and shareholders' equity. As is commonly known, assets must equal liabilities plus equity. The assets section begins with cash and equivalents, which should equal the balance found at the end of the cash flow statement. The balance sheet then displays the changes in each major account. Net income from the income statement flows into the balance sheet as a change in retained earnings (adjusted for payment of dividends).

Key features:

- Shows the financial position of a business
- Expressed as a "snapshot" or financial picture of the company at a specified point in time (i.e., as of December 12, 2022)
- Has three sections: assets, liabilities, and shareholders' equity
- Assets = Liabilities + Shareholders Equity

Cash Flow Statement

The cash flow statement takes net income and adjusts it for any non-cash expenses. Then cash inflows and outflows are calculated using changes in the balance sheet. The cash flow statement displays the change in cash per period, as well as the beginning and ending balance of cash.

Key features:

- Shows the increases and decreases in cash
- Expressed over a period of time, an accounting period (i.e., 1 year, 1 quarter, Year-to-Date, etc.)
- Undoes accrual accounting principles to show pure cash movements
- Has three sections: cash from operations, cash used in investing, and cash from financing
- Shows the net change in the cash balance from start to end of the period

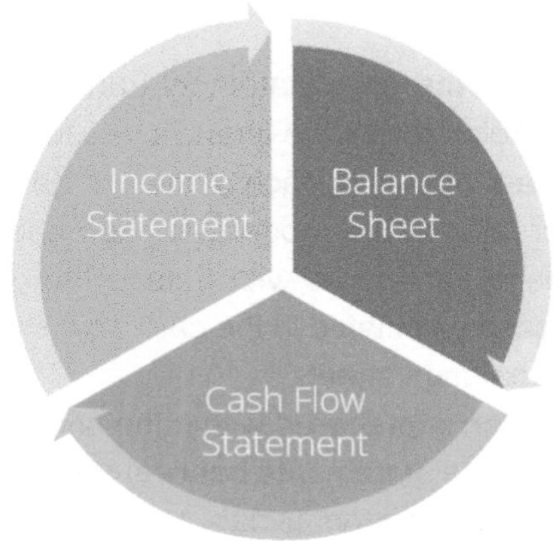

Source: Certified Financial Institute

THE 3 STATEMENTS ARE INTRICATELY LINKED

	Income Statement	Balance Sheet	Cash Flow
Time	Period of time	A point in time	Period of time
Purpose	Profitability	Financial position	Cash movements
Measures	Revenue, expenses, profitability	Assets, liabilities, shareholders' equity	Increases and decreases in cash
Starting Point	Revenue	Cash balance	Net income
Ending Point	Net income	Retained earnings	Cash balance

Source: Certified Financial Institute

These three core statements are intricately linked to one another, and this guide will explain how they all fit together. By following the steps below, you'll be able to connect the three statements on your own.

How Are These Three Core Statements Used in Financial Modeling?

As explained, each of the three financial statements has an interplay of information, and the trends in the relationships of information in these statements, as well as the trends between periods in historical data, are used to forecast future performance.

The preparation and presentation of this information can become quite complicated. In general, however, the following steps are followed to create a financial model:

- Line items for each of the core statements are set up. This provides the overall format and skeleton that the financial model will flesh out.
- Historical numbers are placed in each of the line items.
- At this point, the creator of the model will often check to make sure each of the core statements reconciles with data in the other. For example, the ending balance of cash calculated in the cash flow statement must equal the cash amount in the balance sheet.
- An assumptions section is prepared within the sheet to analyze the trend in each line item of the core statements between periods.
- Assumptions from existing historical data are then used to create forecasted assumptions for the same line items.

FINANCIAL STATEMENTS	Historical Results 2012	2013	2014	2015	2016	2017
Income Statement						
Revenue	**102,007**	**118,086**	**131,345**	**142,341**	**150,772**	**158,311**
Cost of Goods Sold (COGS)	39,023	48,004	49,123	52,654	56,710	58,575
Gross Profit	**62,984**	**70,082**	**82,222**	**89,687**	**94,062**	**99,736**
Expenses						
Salaries and Benefits	26,427	22,658	23,872	23,002	25,245	26,913
Rent and Overhead	10,963	10,125	10,087	11,020	11,412	10,000
Depreciation & Amortization	19,500	18,150	17,205	16,544	16,080	15,008
Interest	2,500	2,500	1,500	1,500	1,500	1,500
Total Expenses	**59,390**	**53,433**	**52,664**	**52,066**	**54,237**	**53,421**
Earnings Before Tax	**3,594**	**16,649**	**29,558**	**37,622**	**39,825**	**46,314**
Taxes	1,120	4,858	8,483	10,908	11,598	12,968
Net Earnings	**2,474**	**11,791**	**21,075**	**26,713**	**28,227**	**33,346**
Balance Sheet						
Assets						
Cash	167,971	181,210	183,715	211,069	239,550	272,530
Accounts Receivable	5,100	5,904	6,567	7,117	7,539	7,807
Inventory	7,805	9,601	9,825	10,531	11,342	11,715
Property & Equipment	45,500	42,350	40,145	38,602	37,521	37,513
Total Assets	**226,376**	**239,065**	**240,252**	**267,319**	**295,951**	**329,564**
Liabilities						
Accounts Payable	3,902	4,800	4,912	5,265	5,671	5,938
Debt	50,000	50,000	30,000	30,000	30,000	30,000
Total Liabilities	**53,902**	**54,800**	**34,912**	**35,265**	**35,671**	**35,938**
Shareholder's Equity						
Equity Capital	170,000	170,000	170,000	170,000	170,000	170,000
Retained Earnings	2,474	14,265	35,340	62,053	90,280	123,627
Shareholder's Equity	**172,474**	**184,265**	**205,340**	**232,053**	**260,280**	**293,627**
Total Liabilities & Shareholder'	**226,376**	**239,065**	**240,252**	**267,319**	**295,951**	**329,564**
Cash Flow Statement						
Operating Cash Flow						
Net Earnings	2,474	11,791	21,075	26,713	28,227	33,346
Plus: Depreciation & Amortization	19,500	18,150	17,205	16,544	16,080	15,008
Less: Changes in Working Capital	9,003	1,702	775	903	827	375
Cash from Operations	**12,971**	**28,239**	**37,505**	**42,354**	**43,480**	**47,980**
Investing Cash Flow						
Investments in Property & Equipment	15,000	15,000	15,000	15,000	15,000	15,000
Cash from Investing	**15,000**	**15,000**	**15,000**	**15,000**	**15,000**	**15,000**
Financing Cash Flow						
Issuance (repayment) of debt	-	-	(20,000)	-	-	-
Issuance (repayment) of equity	170,000	-	-	-	-	-
Cash from Financing	**170,000**	**-**	**(20,000)**	**-**	**-**	**-**
Net Increase (decrease) in Cash	167,971	13,239	2,505	27,354	28,480	32,980
Opening Cash Balance	-	167,971	181,210	183,715	211,069	239,550
Closing Cash Balance	**167,971**	**181,210**	**183,715**	**211,069**	**239,550**	**272,530**

Source: Certified Financial Institute

- The forecasted section of each core statement will use the forecasted assumptions to populate values for each line item. Since the analyst or user has analyzed past trends in creating the forecasted assumptions, the populated values should follow historical trends.
- Supporting schedules are used to calculate more complex line items. For example, the debt schedule is used to calculate interest expense and the balance of debt items. The depreciation and amortization schedule is used to calculate depreciation expense and the balance of long-term fixed assets. These values will flow into the three main statements.

© Corporate Finance Institute®. All rights reserved.	Historical Results					Forecast Period				
FINANCIAL STATEMENTS	2012	2013	2014	2015	2016	2017	2018	2019	2020	2021
Balance Sheet Check	OK	OK	OK	OK	OK	OK	OK	OK	OK	OK
Assumptions										
Income Statement										
Balance Sheet										
Assets										
Cash	167,971	181,210	183,715	211,069	239,550	272,530	307,632	327,097	368,487	413,243
Accounts Receivable	5,100	5,904	6,567	7,117	7,539	7,807	8,158	8,485	8,782	9,045
Inventory	7,805	9,601	9,825	10,531	11,342	11,715	12,242	12,388	12,821	12,839
Property & Equipment	45,500	42,350	40,145	38,602	37,521	37,513	37,508	37,505	37,503	37,502
Total Assets	**226,376**	**239,065**	**240,252**	**267,319**	**295,951**	**329,564**	**365,540**	**385,474**	**427,592**	**472,629**
Liabilities										
Accounts Payable	3,902	4,800	4,912	5,265	5,671	5,938	6,205	6,279	6,498	6,507
Debt	50,000	50,000	30,000	30,000	30,000	30,000	30,000	10,000	10,000	10,000
Total Liabilities	**53,902**	**54,800**	**34,912**	**35,265**	**35,671**	**35,938**	**36,205**	**16,279**	**16,498**	**16,507**
Shareholder's Equity										
Equity Capital	170,000	170,000	170,000	170,000	170,000	170,000	170,000	170,000	170,000	170,000
Retained Earnings	2,474	14,265	35,340	62,053	90,280	123,627	159,335	199,195	241,094	286,122
Shareholder's Equity	**172,474**	**184,265**	**205,340**	**232,053**	**260,280**	**293,627**	**329,335**	**369,195**	**411,094**	**456,122**
Total Liabilities & Shareholder's Equity	**226,376**	**239,065**	**240,252**	**267,319**	**295,951**	**329,564**	**365,540**	**385,474**	**427,592**	**472,629**
Check	*0.000*	*0.000*	*0.000*	*0.000*	*0.000*	*0.000*	*0.000*	*0.000*	*0.000*	*0.000*
Cash Flow Statement										
Supporting Schedules										

Source: Certified Financial Institute

Financial Courses for the Nonfinancial

If you are one of the right-brained many who lack financial skills, you can take an online course to get up to speed. This is akin to a left-brainer needing to understand spatial concepts, colors, and wordsmithing… a color-by-numbers course.

There are several good courses available for the nonfinancial individual that explain the key financial concepts, tools, and techniques to help you build and develop the proficiencies you need. I like the ones Certified Financial Institute offers. They have two free courses that do a superb job of teaching the basics:

- Accounting Fundamentals
- Reading Financial Statements

CFI offers other free financial courses. If you want to learn more, check them out in Resources here: www.BrainToBank.com/Resources.

Human vs. Software: Which Accounting Method Is Right for You?

As you start working with your financials, you will want to make sure the methods you use to track expenses, income, and taxes are robust yet manageable. While accounting software can be beneficial and efficient, it is still relatively new.

For decades, small business owners and entrepreneurs have taken advantage of Certified Public Accountant (CPA) services to help track their expenses, produce reports, handle payments, and prepare taxes.

As you bring your idea from brain to bank, you will want to make sure you have your accounting needs covered. Which solution is better: human accountant or software? Let's break down some of the critical aspects of accounting and compare each option.

Usability

Personal Accountant: The best part of hiring a professional accountant is that a CPA has the training and experience to handle all the details for you. An accountant will work on your behalf to track and prepare financial information and help you understand the various forms and reports the CPA creates.

Accounting Software: While accounting software can handle nearly all of the services a CPA covers, there will be a learning curve while you become familiar with the system. However, most accounting software comes with training guides and videos to help you learn the ropes quickly.

Cost

Personal Accountant: Hiring a personal accountant can get expensive quickly. Depending on the services the CPA is handling for you and your business, keeping one on retainer can cost hundreds to thousands of dollars. Fortunately, these costs are typically tax-deductible.

Accounting Software: Most software solutions require a purchase price and subscription price. Depending on the product and the services provided, the costs may vary. However, using software is often much more cost-effective than hiring a professional accountant.

Security

Personal Accountant: Personal accountants are often a safe and secure way to handle your classified financial information. While there are always instances of an accountant committing fraud, you can usually avoid the unthinkable if you do your due diligence in investigating the professional records and ratings of potential personal accountants and then choosing wisely.

Accounting Software: Because accounting software is data-dependent, you may be at risk of losing data or being hacked. Thankfully, accounting software continues to evolve and advance, and security is becoming a more critical aspect of that — helping protect you and your data from loss or theft.

Experience

Personal Accountant: If you are comfortable working with an individual or team, you may enjoy having a human accountant more than navigating a digital accounting program.

Accounting Software: Many business owners love the ability to handle their financials in-house with software solutions. If you are savvy and understand how to use these tools, software may make the accounting process much more convenient.

Choose the Accounting That's Right for YOU

The most important thing is that you are consistently and actively keeping track of your financials. Many entrepreneurs go wrong when they lose sight of their current finances while working hard to bring their idea to life.

Choose the method you are most comfortable with, and keep at it with clarity, consistency, and transparency.

If you like the idea of having a trained and experienced individual looking over your money and keeping you updated with industry insights, then a CPA may be the right fit for you. A CPA can also certify whether your accounting is completed by Generally Accepted Accounting Principles (GAAP).

Not too worried about having human opinion and guidance, yet want the ability to look up your current finances and make data-driven decisions quickly? Choose one of the innovative software solutions we have listed below.

CHOOSING AN ACCOUNTING SOFTWARE

In the olden days, keeping "the books" for a business involved reams of paper, lots of ledgers, and large bottles of aspirin. Now, as with most business software services, there are many online, paperless accounting platforms to choose from when it comes to needing to track your company's finances.

In my opinion, QuickBooks is still the best online accounting application for small businesses. It's easy to use, well designed, and can cater to many different industries. It's more expensive than some of the other similar SaaS products, but in the long run, it does a superb job.

There are plenty of free bookkeeping tools on the market, but most small businesses should be distrustful of "free" programs to which they will be exposing their financial data.

There is a reputable free version of QuickBooks available that allows you to create invoices, print checks, handle payroll, and manage up to 20 customer accounts. QuickBooks is the best option for growing companies, in fact, because it's easy to step up to the paid version, which lets users track more than 10,000 customers... a problem we all hope to have.

Check out other online accounting software suggestions here:
www.BrainToBank.com/Resources.

CHAPTER 6 - Action Accelerators

Take action on these items NOW to keep driving your idea from Brain to Bank:

1. If you are not already acquainted with business finance, take these two free short courses online at Corporate Finance Institute:
   Accounting Fundamentals
   Reading Financial Statements

2. If you already have accounting software, that's great. If not, choose a platform, log in, and set up your company. You can set up your account categories or hire a virtual assistant to do it for you. Either way, start today and keep your books current at all times. You can get a free trial of many popular accounting software programs. Some of the platforms I like and use are listed here: www.BrainToBank.com/Resources.

3. Set up a system for implementing and overseeing financial activities, including budgets, accounting systems, and financial reporting. Engage competent advisors, conduct periodic reviews of the financial status of your company, and maintain proper records. These regular activities will aid you in presenting your company accurately and completely each step of the way.

4. Update your roadmap so it has the most current information.

STICK TO THE PLAN

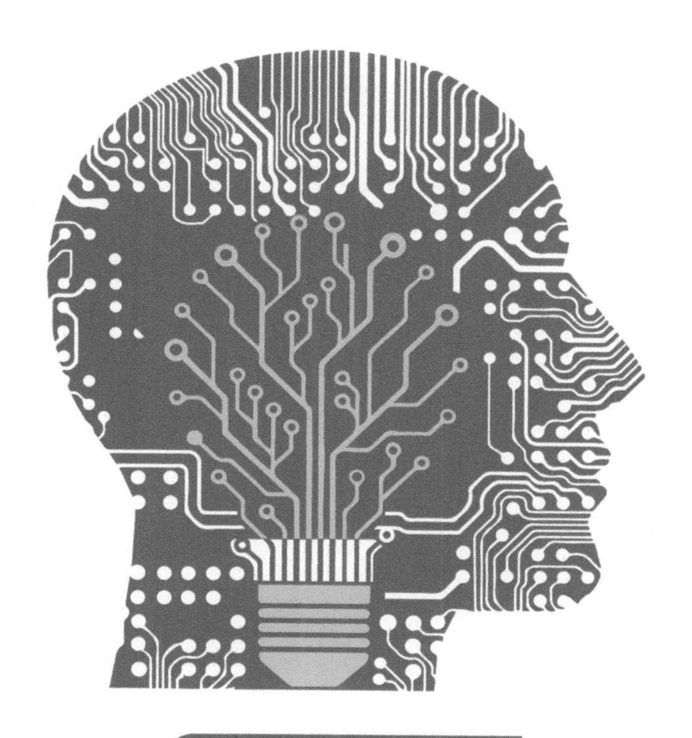

PART TWO

GOING THE DISTANCE

Chapter 7

Working Together Alone

SOLOSOCIALIZING

One day I sat in Starbucks absentmindedly sipping my reg Flat White Grande with one hand and clicking away on my laptop with the other while glancing around at the room packed with similar solos doing the same thing. Most of them were wearing headsets and obviously ignoring... or wanting to ignore... all that was around them.

I fit right in. I had come here to work and to solosocialize... ignore everyone around me while feeling I was part of a group and immersed in the company of others.

Solosocializing is what we do when we go to a crowded place to be alone. Most of us have no intention of talking or engaging with anyone there except to place our coffee order:

"I'll have a quad long-shot Grande in a Venti cup, half-caf double cupped no sleeve, salted caramel mocha latte with 2 pumps of sugar-free vanilla but if you don't have sugar-free then no vanilla but then add two extra pumps of white mocha, made with soy at 120 degrees and a java chip inclusion with whipped cream. Please."

We don't wait in the pick-up line to grab our order the minute it's up because we might get stuck talking to someone we don't know, so we hustle back to our tables. Mindlessly, we lamely begin the task of getting our products from mind to market while listening for our names to be called.

We like being there by ourselves. It gives us the freedom to get stuff done without interference, yet we're not completely alone.

Being a one-person business, a.k.a. solopreneur, is much the same. We like being the creator of our new product. We like doing it our way and making the decisions, whether good or not-so-good, and we relish the ability to bring on other contributors when and how needed. Alone.

I've been conducting business this way my entire life. It works for me. It will work for you too if working together alone is your preferred modus operandi.

WHY GOING SOLO IS THE NEW COOL

There are days when you spend a lot of time at your coffee hangout of choice. And then there are times when you spend the entire day on the phone, in appointments, and in meetings you'd rather not attend. These are the days you hustle through each event, one after another, eating a half-devoured nutrition bar just to keep going. At the end of the day or night, you're exhausted, a spent mayfly dangling on the end of the line.

Then there are those glorious days when you have an entire "office day." Alone. The only person you talk to is yourself as your mind's self-chatter explodes into a million prismatic wavelengths, energizing you with new ideas, problem-solving eurekas, and excess energy you later need to burn off with a second workout. You talk to no one. Well... maybe you break down and give an occasional shout-out to Siri or Alexa or Google, but mostly... it's just you. You get stuff done. Lots of stuff. Because you can.

However, being a one-person business, a.k.a. solopreneur, doesn't mean you're the only one working in your business. It means you are the core – the center – of all that happens, like the hub of a many-spoked wheel racing down the highway of entrepreneurship. All of the various components that go into creating and maintaining this multi-dimensional wheel are linked to you, but they operate independently as each spoke completes a very specific task or set of tasks.

Few companies, especially start-ups, are able to fulfill all of the needed processes and systems in-house... which usually means by you.

For example, you know you need to create a website, or at least a landing page, for your new business to promote your product or service. You suck at web design, and you don't want to spend endless hours on web template platforms watching how to "easily" put together your website via WordPress, which is once again something you have to Google several times to figure out.

Like a DC Comics crime victim, you wholeheartedly embrace the idea of a flowing-caped superhero flying to your rescue and completing this much-needed yet dreaded chore.

ENTER: Outsourcing.

The art of outsourcing includes working with people you know in accounting, graphic design, branding and marketing, video, editing, and endless other niche industries.

It also includes working with people you don't know, such as domestic and global Virtual Assistants (commonly referred to as VAs). Don't worry, you won't need to learn foreign languages or experience culture shock in any way… although you will need to work around various global time zones occasionally.

You will for sure need to fine-tune your communication skills. More on this in a minute.

Here's the coolest part about outsourcing: subcontracting needed areas of business and product development ensures the probability of working with competent individuals for those particular processes. It also eliminates mistakes one might make while trying to save money by doing things not even a video on YouTube could adequately teach.

This is truly the best way to work if you don't want to wear 50 hats and wonder *when oh when* is this going to get easier?

Hiring remote workers and VAs may seem like an unnecessary expense, especially if you are still trying to get your new company up and running.

But know this: It has been estimated that hiring virtual assistants can save you as much as 40 percent in business expenses. These savings can then be allocated to other areas of your business.

Yeah baby, take that one to the bank!

Outsourcing – Who Not How

When multiple tasks simultaneously arise like swarming bees from an overcrowded hive, the first question we usually ask ourselves is: "HOW will I get all of this done?" The good news is, you now have a new question you'll ask yourself: "WHO can I outsource this to?"

A great read on the art of delegating is the book *Who Not How* by Dan Sullivan and Dr. Benjamin Hardy. The authors state: "Making this shift involves retraining your brain to stop limiting your potential based on what you can do on your own and instead focus on the infinite and endless connections between yourself and other people as well as the limitless transformation possible through those connections."[15]

For more than a decade I consulted for veterinary clinics, creating more efficient and effective processes and systems for their businesses. I quickly learned that veterinarians were used to doing almost everything themselves, including giving vaccinations, changing bandages, and administering medications. What this meant for the bottom line is their time was used up every day doing tasks that could have been given to assistants, kennel attendants, and other workers at the clinic.

The first piece of advice I'd give medical professionals — or any other type of professional — to help their practice become more profitable is this: never do a task you can delegate. Your only tasks and duties are those that require your specific degree, certification, and license to complete the task.

It is even more critical for entrepreneurs — especially solopreneurs — to outsource everything that does not involve major decisions and the core competencies that are the strategic focus of the business. This maximizes profitability by keeping you, the CEO and backbone of the company spending time *on* the business, not *in* the business.

If you hire and then manage your outsourced workers correctly, you will reap the benefits of selective delegation in many ways:

- Virtual Assistants are hired on a contractual basis and therefore are easily terminated and replaced if they don't work out.
- Many of the freelancers you hire may be overseas, which means they will get work done while you sleep. Give them your instructions for the next day at the end of your day, and when you wake up, *voilà!* The work is in your inbox.

- You won't need to spend a lot of time training your virtual assistant because you have already chosen a pro who knows how to get the job done. Your ability to communicate a job succinctly and accurately is the key to shortening the amount of time they need to complete it.

Outsourcing - The First Step Toward Growth

As you can see, outsourcing can be one of the best ways to start offloading tasks and work you don't have the bandwidth to complete.

Here's a truth about using unknown freelancers: you may initially have to work through a couple of inexperienced or dishonest hires before you find one that truly fits your niche and needs. Keep in mind freelancers and contractors come in all shapes, sizes, and skill levels so you will need to prepare for the possibility that a few may not offer the exact services you seek.

If you are going to grow your business, then you will eventually need to build a team around you and your idea. As an entrepreneur, outsourcing work or specific tasks is a great way to dip your feet into the realm of growth and scaling your business.

If you have been operating as a one-person show so far (a.k.a. solopreneur), this may be the first time you have handed a portion of your project to someone else. Stop and take a deep breath and have faith in the outsourcing system. Nine times out of 10, my freelancers have become committed, passionate partners in my entrepreneurial journey. Why? Because they are small business owners just like me, so they have a vested interest in my success as well as their own. This is one of the many advantages of the aforementioned symbiotic relationship called win/win.

Freelance entrepreneurs are working their tails off just like you to try and bring their own ideas to the market. Their product may be different from yours — graphic design, copywriting, social media content curation — but they are traveling down the same road as you to see their own ideas come to life.

Have I occasionally had a rough experience with freelancers? Yes; I even had to fire a few as they hadn't been honest about their ability to produce the product I had paid them for. That's okay, because it's still worth the risk. The majority of those offering services have been more than competent to give me what I needed and have saved me large swaths of time I'd have spent first learning how to do it and then doing it. Yes, time is money.

If you see your freelancer or VA as a partner rather than an employee, you will begin to build a managerial presence others will want to follow and support. Treat these workers well and invite them into your process and you will find invaluable partners throughout the rest of your journey.

With any luck, you will begin to build skills and abilities in leading others that will pay off massively in the days ahead. When the moment comes when you are ready to scale your business from solopreneur to enterprise, you will look back on your early days of outsourcing with thankfulness. And most likely, you'll continue to maintain some outsourcing partners on a regular basis, because it will still be an efficient and effective thing to do.

Running a business using online services and collaborators is a great way to get things done and add much-needed resources to your team — whether permanently or just for one project.

Some of the platforms I like and use are listed here:
www.BrainToBank.com/Resources.

You don't have to choose one platform... try several, to find which ones fit your budget and also give you quality outsourced results.

Do delegate. Do outsource. It will preserve your sanity.

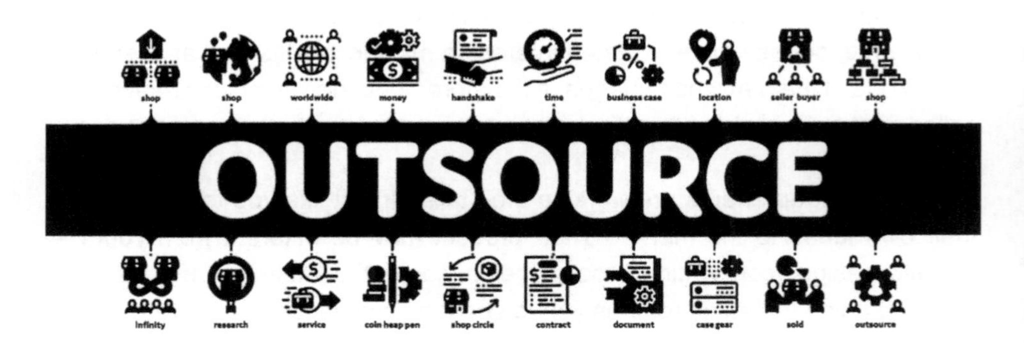

WHAT TO OUTSOURCE

Outsourcing nonessential tasks that have occupied much of your time will free you up to do more "executive-type" work such as strategic planning, weighing in on marketing campaigns, and developing tactics for customer relations and retention. You can delegate many nonessentials such as these:

- Phone call coverage
- Email filtering
- Calendar management
- Appointment setting
- Customer Relationship Management (CRM) updates
- Social media management
- Payroll preparation
- Bookkeeping
- Website design and development
- Search Engine Optimization (SEO)
- Content management services
- Digital marketing
- Blogging
- Software development
- Medical, legal, and audio transcription
- Translation services
- Inventory management
- Data protection and security
- Market research

This is the short list. Even though you most likely have the skills to do all or most of these tasks, you won't have the time if you are truly focused on profit-generating activities.

GREAT COMMUNICATION IS VITAL

The key to working with remote teammates is communication. Poor communication will crash your project faster than your mother walking in on a "my parents are away on vacation" teenage party. Communication is the key to getting what you want, how you want, and when you want.

Great, not good, communication allows you to streamline processes, gaining efficiency and effectiveness with better results, on time and in budget. In short, communication can either make or break getting your project to market in a timely manner, so you want to fine-tune your ability to let others know exactly what you need and expect. If they don't understand, that's on you.

Communication is even more important when you are not working in a face-to-face environment, but virtually. Without clear, concise, and detailed communication telling employees what you want by when and how, you are wasting time and money, not to mention the headaches you'll get from banging your head against the wall in frustration. The "lost in translation" factor alone is enough to make you want to go back to your paper route, when things were easy and a nap would make up for having to get up at 4:00 am.

To successfully utilize online and remote virtual assistants, you must at all times be able to communicate effectively, or you will not get the results you are expecting. Then you'll have to start over, as in a bad game of *Mother May I?* where you take one step forward and two steps back. Time waster, money flusher, efficiency killer.

The first thing to do is make sure your freelancer has English skills. The problem with many virtual assistants offering their services is they list themselves as native English speakers, but they may or may not be.

Sometimes a resume's language skills category will use the grouping *Native or Bilingual*, so that's a possible explanation. Otherwise, you may need to do further investigation.

When outsourcing to a freelancer I've never worked with before, I will research sellers who have successfully completed multiple contracts and gained high ratings. Typically, I use the "Contact Seller" button to check the level of their language expertise. You can email sellers you are considering a message asking a few questions and see how they reply. Even in a short sentence, you can usually tell how well-honed their language skills are.

If they respond to a complex question with just two to four words, they could be avoiding long discussions, and you should most likely pass.

There is also the user of Google Translate, who will usually in the end frustrate and ultimately disappoint you. Their skills are most likely self-listed as Basic, or worse, Unspecified.

Look for the individuals who are:

- Conversational
- Fluent
- Native or Bilingual

I have had good luck with English speakers who are conversational when the project is graphic design, video, or otherwise arts-related. But I would not choose a freelancer claiming basic or conversational command of English for tasks involving text or copywriting or editing.

You can always choose a freelancer who is from the U.S. or United Kingdom, but it is not always necessary. Plus, their rates are usually much higher, and for a start-up with limited funds and a tight budget every dollar counts. Still, you can use filters to help you "up" the chance of getting a person with great English skills if you are needing writing, editing, or anything else requiring linguistic expertise.

Things to include in your communication to your freelancer:

1. **Scope** - for example:
   Hi Ibrahim: I hope you are doing well! I'm getting ready to record about 20 videos in Camtasia for a training project. If I record them with a green screen background, can you drop in a different background on each one? Each video will be 7 minutes or less. Please let me know if you can do this and time and cost. Thanks!

2. **Time** - the due date. The major online freelancer portals have a built-in day and time where you can always see when the project is due. There are penalties for Sellers who miss the deadline, so no need to micro-manage them daily, as they are already motivated to avoid negative points on their record.

   Watch out for workers who have procrastinated and on the last day in the last hour want you to extend the deadline so they are not penalized by the platform. Make it very clear when you hire them that you will not extend the deadline and when the project is due it really is due. Mark this date on your calendar so you can make sure the due date target is hit on time.

3. **Cost** – your budget. You will know the cost of the project if it is a flat-rate pricing structure before the freelancer even starts because your money to pay him or her (not including fees or a tip) will be held in escrow by the company. For example, if I order a gig on Fiverr for graphic design, I know what the seller is charging me... let's say it's $35, plus Fiverr will charge me

a flat service fee. This sum is what you will pay in advance to Fiverr. They in turn will release the money to the freelancer if and only if you approve the final delivery.

In my initial communication with a seller, I always add detailed bullet points of what I need them to do. I have my expectations in writing before I ever order and pay for the work, in case I need that info later to compare it with the final delivery.

When you order your gig, you will have the opportunity to reiterate what you have already agreed upon. I include my initial communication plus any files in the follow-up request for project details. This triggers the freelancer to begin the project.

When hiring someone you've never worked with, keep the first project you give to them a small task. Don't hire a new virtual assistant and dump 40 hours' worth of work on him/her just because you feel compelled to get all that strangling and stressful stuff off your own plate. Take it slow with a newbie. Test whether this hire is a good fit for you, is efficient and effective, and someone you want to work with regularly.

HIRING REMOTE WORKERS AND VIRTUAL ASSISTANTS

Here's the way it usually proceeds:

You contact the seller before you place your order. You want to make sure they can do what you need with expertise and deliver on time. As an example, here's how I communicate with a seller I have used for years. He's my video editing guy based overseas:

Me Jun 25, 12:31 PM

Hi Ibrahim:

I hope you're doing great! I need some minor video editing on 30 short video modules. I need to take the logo off the back end so a company can white label the series. Can you do this for me? If so, by when?

Ibrahim_isi Jun 25, 2:11 PM

Hi River, thanks for contacting me again, yes I can help you to remove the logo, let me know your budget for all 30 videos, then I will send the offer, and let's start.

Me Jun 25, 2:27 PM

I don't have an idea of cost. Please suggest. It is a simple deletion at the end.

Note: It's better to get the seller to tell you a price first; then you have an idea of how to negotiate.

Ibrahim_isi Jun 25, 2:29 PM

yes, I see, $40 is Okay ?

Me Jun 25, 2:30 PM

For all 30 videos?

Ibrahim_isi Jun 25, 2:32 PM

yes all videos

Me Jun 25, 7:27 PM

Yes, okay. Please send custom order. Thx.

For the next step, you will place your order when the custom offer is sent. An example of what this looks like is below:

Here's your Custom Offer

$40

I will do professional video editing within 48 hours

Your Offer includes

2-Day Delivery

You will pay before your freelancer starts the work. There are the seller's fees plus the platform fee. For example, this order breaks down as follows:

Professional video editing within 48 hours

2 days $40

SUBTOTAL $40

SERVICE FEE $2 (platform service fee)

TOTAL $42

At this point, you submit your final requirements. This includes any other details you need to communicate as well as files and links such as a Dropbox or Google Docs folder.

Me

Thanks Ibrahim. Please make sure to complete this in 2 days. Let me know if you have any questions.

Thanks. River

Next steps:

Your order starts:

Your order started *Jun 26, 08:56 AM*

Your delivery date was updated to June 28 *Jun 26, 08:56 AM*

Then your order is complete.

Ibrahim_isi Jun 28, 08:52 AM

Hello River,

Here are all videos, check it out.

www.drive.google.com/drive

Feel free to ask to edit it further, as you need.

If the video is okay. Please mark the order as completed and support me with review.

Thanks, and have a great day! :)

Ibrahim

You review the work and make sure it is what you asked for, and if not, you don't accept the delivery and ask for revisions. Communication is vital in getting the details of your project completed the way you envisioned. I take a screenshot and mark it up to help clarify what is not correct. Fiverr has a built-in view and mark system that works great, so you can do this right on the platform if you want.

After you get your delivery just the way you want, you accept it. Then you leave a review of their work. You will rate up to 5 stars for each:

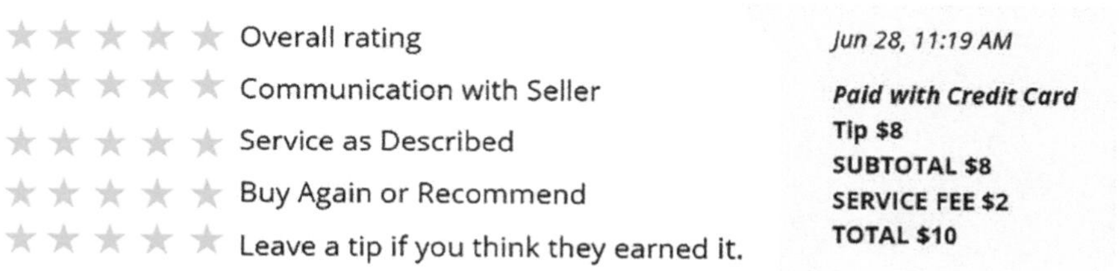

★★★★★ Overall rating
★★★★★ Communication with Seller
★★★★★ Service as Described
★★★★★ Buy Again or Recommend
★★★★★ Leave a tip if you think they earned it.

Jun 28, 11:19 AM

Paid with Credit Card
Tip $8
SUBTOTAL $8
SERVICE FEE $2
TOTAL $10

Note: *For Sellers who do a great job I always leave a tip and a glowing 5-star review. I tell them what a great job they did, what they did that was exceptional, and that I intend to use them again. And then I do. This does two things: (1) It makes them feel good about their work and working with me; (2) They are eager to work with me again and will put my order ahead of others to please me next time I contact them.*

To break down the effectiveness and efficiency of using this seller, in two days I received 30 edited videos for a total of $62.00 or $2.06 for each video. It was a sweet deal.

Now I could have gone into a software program on my computer and tried to figure out how to do this myself and save the $62.00, but it would have taken me days to learn how to do it and then who knows how it would have looked, as I am not a professional. Additionally, I was able to use those two days to do other things only I can do, things I cannot farm out to anyone else.

This is the beauty of leveraging your virtual assistants to save you time, money, and most often frustration. Most importantly, you are getting the work done by true professionals, so the output and results of the work exceed the sum of the parts. Brilliant, right?

Cultivate your relationships with those who deliver great work on time and within budget. Hang on to these reliable individuals and companies, as they are hard to find, but once you do, they will work hard and fast for you.

Properly developed, a virtual assistant can become a key advantage in building your business while leaving you to deal with the big-picture items. A virtual assistant is an asset who can lower your business costs significantly without compromising your productivity. In fact, your assistants will increase productivity exponentially if you choose and manage them properly.

CHAPTER 7 - Action Accelerators

THINK IT → ORGANIZE IT → DO IT

Take action on these items NOW to keep driving your idea from Brain to Bank:

1. Go to your favorite coffee shop and order the most obnoxious drink you can imagine. Just kidding, but you get extra credit if you really do this.

2. Check out at least three freelancer websites. I recommend one of them be Fiverr, as it is easily navigable, cheap to play on, and they are ever-progressive in their enhancements and advancements.

3. Choose at least three things you will outsource to make your life easier. Choose from the following list or create three of your own items:

    - Phone call coverage
    - Email filtering
    - Calendar management
    - Appointment setting
    - CRM updates
    - Social media management
    - Bill pay and payroll preparation
    - Bookkeeping
    - Website design and development
    - SEO
    - Content management services
    - Digital marketing
    - Blogging
    - Software development
    - Medical, legal and audio Transcription
    - Translation services
    - Inventory management
    - Data protection and security
    - Market research

4. Hire three different freelancers (it doesn't matter if they are on the same platform) and learn the ropes of communicating and working with them.

5. Enjoy the freedom of freelancers and outsourcing.

6. Update your roadmap so it has the most current information.

STICK TO THE PLAN

Chapter 8

Create Exit Strategies

PERMANENT PIT STOPS

Most inventors and innovators dream of eventually selling their genius creation and business. Then they will bask in the glory of a Caribbean beach, tanning themselves in a sun that never quits shining. If this is the dream, or something similar, that gets you out of bed in the morning and slaying those dragons, then planning for an eventual exit is essential. You should be ready to make a permanent pit stop and trade drivers, knowing your replacement is well-positioned to still win the race.

Another Episode in the Entrepreneur Drama Series
I Didn't See It Coming

I recently worked with a company that created a Doing Business As (DBA) for an auxiliary service they were adding to their stable. Doing things this way meant the parent company was still on many levels essentially involved in the day-to-day operations and financials of this new enterprise.

The owners didn't realize at the time, and who does, that their new enterprise was going to be a great success and would one day become a spin-off (a spin-off is the creation of an independent company through the sale or distribution of new shares of an existing business or division of a parent company).

Consequently, because the owners had not planned an exit strategy for this add-on company, when it came time to sell it, they had a big mess on their hands. They had to unmingle financial records, untangle tax implications, and form a new LLC that could be acquired in the upcoming transaction as an independent business. The DBA had some employees who worked only for the service company, while others worked for both companies. What to do here?

In short, the owners had not treated the new DBA as a separate entity from the beginning, and therefore a lot of work was required to produce the correct information needed by the potential buyers.

A successful exit strategy pays you back the time, money, blood, and sweat (and maybe tears) you put into your product and business. It is vital to your success.

Creating an exit strategy isn't usually the first thing entrepreneurs think about when considering how to get their product from concept to cash. Very few entrepreneurs who enter the game of getting ideas from concept to commercialization entertain the thought of running their new business for the rest of their lives; they don't intend to make it their everything. Most often, the product is a project. In other words, it has a beginning and an end when it comes to the amount of time you're willing to invest.

So, here's the thing to remember: Every decision you make from day one until you decide to exit — whether it be by sale, merger, acquisition, IPO, or liquidation — will ultimately affect your exit and the subsequent cash you'll receive. Having a solid plan in place helps guarantee a prosperous financial future and catching a fast boat to your exotic island.

So, You Wanna Get "Bought Out"?

Many an entrepreneur's dream is to create the next best innovative company or product that catches the eye of a major company flush with cash. The formula seems simple enough:

Step 1: You bring your incredible idea from brain to bank.

Step 2: You are successful with your market idea, and Google or Apple representatives call you with an offer to buy your company.

Step 3: You make the sale and are now a mega-millionaire success story ready to launch your next big idea, or become an investor on Shark Tank for aspiring entrepreneurs, or retire at a young age and head out on the start-up speaking circuit.

Big Bucks for Big Ideas

You've likely been inspired by the stories of successful company purchases such as the social media app Instagram being bought by Facebook for $1 billion or Google acquiring the digital thermostat company Nest for $3.2 billion.

These are tremendous stories because they are relatively rare occurrences. However, there are a few ways you can set yourself apart from your competitors and potentially catch the attention of a tech giant:

1. Make sure you KNOW and OWN the WHY behind your product throughout your development process. Investors won't give you a second thought if you can't prove to them you are confident in your idea.
2. Create an innovative product.
3. The market may not think it's necessary today, but tomorrow the world won't be able to live without it. Once, nobody felt the need to post a daily filtered photo of their breakfast, but along came Instagram, and here we are. Cheerios. Again. Really?
4. Invest in your (and their) potential scalability. Not only do investors or business giants want a great product, they want a product they can quickly scale into their business models. If you can prove your product fits a more prominent company's needs, this can help you get noticed and hopefully get that first meeting.
5. Consider building up your resources. While some unicorns are simply too good to pass up, many investors want to see a bit of flesh in the game before they make a move. If you can start raising some funds on your end, you will increase your chances of being noticed.
6. Network, network, network. Much of this process is similar to finding co-founders or partners in your early stage of bringing an idea to market. Never stop networking throughout your journey - you never know when you may cross paths with someone ready to pull out a checkbook and buy you out.

A Lot of Work - Even More Luck

Here's the hard reality: there is no guaranteed way to ensure that your exit strategy includes being handed a million- or billion-dollar payout for your idea. If you start with the expectation that you are going to be bought out, you may find yourself dealing with disappointment quickly.

Don't let the idea of money or retirement cause you to forget why you got involved in business in the first place: to bring your idea to life and see your dreams come true in an authentic way. This is the true feeling of satisfaction you should have no matter your exit.

DEVELOPING YOUR EXIT PLAN

Where to begin? Start by deciding:

- How long do you want to stay involved in your business?
- What are your financial goals... both personal and business?
- Do you have investors or creditors you'll need to pay off before exiting?

Next, investigate your available exit options:

Liquidation

This exit plan is fully executed when you simply one day place a "CLOSED" sign in the window and ride off into the sunset. However, you will need to take care that all of your creditors and shareholders have been paid. Otherwise, you may find them or the authorities storming your private island beach to collect their money.

It's often difficult to close down a business you worked so hard to build, but sometimes it's the most viable way to repay investors and still make money. The liquidation exit method can be done in two different ways:

1. You can liquidate your business over time by implementing what's known as a "lifestyle company." This is a fun strategy, as you live high on the hog today by paying yourself a big salary and lots of bonuses and rewarding yourself with huge dividends via a special class of shares only you possess.

   While you could never get away with this in a public company, private companies have done it for decades. You pay yourself as much as you can until the money runs out. Then you hang your "CLOSED" sign out and hightail it for your sandy hideaway.

The downside of this "high on the hog" technique is that there may be more tax implications than you are aware of down the road. Additionally, if you have investors, not to mention employees, you may make them very unhappy with your "take it now not later" attitude. I do not recommend this strategy.

2. The second option in liquidation is to sell your assets, which may include inventory, equipment, and real estate. You'll also need to pay your creditors and investors before pocketing the leftover cash.

Sale

Selling your business to someone else who can continue your vision is what most owners have in mind when it's time to play more golf or visit the grandkids more often. Your buyer may be a son or daughter, or another family member, a trusted employee, or a customer who's always admired you and how you've built such a great product or service.

Mergers and Acquisitions (M&A)

M&A is one of the most common exit strategies.
A merger occurs when two separate entities combine forces to create a new, joint organization.

Normally, a merger is transacted to decrease operational costs, expand into new markets, and increase revenue and profits. Mergers are typically voluntary, unlike the type of M&A called a hostile takeover. The two companies become a new entity with a new ownership and management configuration, and stock is issued in the name of the new business entity.

An acquisition, on the other hand, involves the takeover of one entity by another. The smaller company is usually dismantled and ceases to exist.
Over the years, however, these terms have become increasingly intermingled and used interchangeably with one another.

You may encounter one of these types of buyers in the M&A arena:

- Financial Buyer
  These buyers are generally classified as investors; their main interest is in

the return they will gain by buying your business. Cash flow is the name of the game for them, as well as gains in a future exit from the business sometime down the road. These buyers are mainly interested in the financial statements of your company, as they are buying future earnings.

- Strategic Buyer
  These buyers are more interested in how your company fits into their long-term business plan for operations and expansion. They are often willing to pay you more for your company, as they may realize synergistic benefits almost immediately. Synergy allows two or more companies to combine to either generate more profits and/or reduce costs together by maximizing economies of scale created from the merger. Strategic buyers believe that combining with your company will give them more benefits than pursuing their goals alone.

  A strategic buyer may also have better access to capital and may offer stock, cash, or a combination of the two in payment for your business.

  The best strategic fit for you may be a buyer who needs your business to expand into a new market, offer a new product to its own existing customers without having to develop it, or simply wants to reduce costs, thus increasing profits.

  In an M&A transaction, other comparable companies help to determine the value of your company. Negotiation plays a part in determining the selling price. If you are lucky enough to have more than one company involved in purchasing yours, an auction or bidding process will ratchet up your price even more, leaving extra cash in your pocket to purchase that helicopter for your island.

IPO

An Initial Public Offering (IPO) refers to the process of offering newly issued stock shares of a private corporation to the public. IPOs are rare compared with the other exit actions mentioned.

This new public share issuance permits a company to raise capital from public investors, making it a public company. The transition from a private to a public company can be a pivotal time for private investors to make some good moolah from their investment if things go well.

But before you get dollar signs in your irises, you should know an IPO is expensive, and the costs of maintaining a public company are ongoing and usually unrelated to the other costs of doing business.

If you are still keen on considering an IPO as your exit strategy, a lot of research and reading is in your future to truly understand what effect it will have on what is currently your small and manageable business.

So, whichever exit strategy you think you may use, prepare your company as if you were going to exit in the near future. This will force you to create the proper systems and processes for a best-practices business today with little effort later if you truly do exit.

CHAPTER 8 - Action Accelerators

THINK IT → ORGANIZE IT → DO IT

Take action on these items NOW to keep driving your idea from Brain to Bank:

1. Considering what you know right now, answer the following questions to the best of your ability:

    - How long do you want to stay involved in your business?

      ____

    - What are your financial goals… both personal and business?

      ____

    - Do you have investors or creditors you'll need to pay off before exiting?

      ____

Prepare your company as if you were going to exit in the near future. This will force you to create the proper systems and processes for a best-practices business today with little effort later if you truly do exit.

2. Whichever exit strategy you are considering, you'll need to do these things now to prepare for the best outcome if and when you exit:

    - Organize your finances. The first step to developing an exit plan is to prepare an accurate account of your finances, both personally and professionally. As previously mentioned, ideally you should do this when you first set up your books, so later you don't have to untangle or, worse, go back and enter your financial data from the beginning.
    - Categorize and file all documents. This includes your legal documents such as the entity registration, licenses, NDAs, and other contracts potential buyers will ask to see. If you create a manageable filing system now, your life will be much easier while you are running your project, not

to speak of when it's time to exit. I scan all of my valuable documents into PDFs and file them electronically in Dropbox in appropriately named folders. This way, I can easily locate and email them when needed. Additionally, you will want to keep hard copies of the original signed documents, such as those pertaining to the final, stamped approval of the organization entity and signed Operating Agreement.

- Choose and develop your leadership team. Develop an organization chart, even if it's just little ole you at the top. Then you'll add others whom you work with regularly, such as your CPA, bookkeeper, graphic designer, video editor, etc. Once you've decided to exit your business, you will be able to transfer your responsibilities to new leadership and deliver information on key providers you've used over the years.

3. Update your roadmap so it has the most current information.

STICK TO THE PLAN

Chapter 9

Patents and Intellectual Property

NOTE: This chapter is more advanced. Please consult the glossary in the back of the book when needed to ward off panic attacks of inadequacy or paralyzing confusion.

WHAT IS IP?

Intellectual property (IP) is the category of property that covers intangible creations of the human intellect. There are many types of IP, including copyrights, patents, trademarks, and trade secrets.

It is strongly advisable to consult an IP attorney to see which types of intellectual property you may need to protect for your product.

The most complicated and costly IP is a patent.[16]

BURN BABY, BURN

Another Episode in the Entrepreneur Drama Series

I Didn't See It Coming

Every year tens of thousands of individuals attempt to develop their products or services and commercially market them. Although a patent can provide valuable protection for a successful invention, getting a patent does not increase your chances of commercial success.

When I was working with a medical device company that was creating a new heart monitoring device, the founders had already applied for, paid for, and were still in the middle of steering more than a dozen patents through the IP obstacle course. They weren't anywhere near completing the process and had already spent over $170,000 when I came onto the scene to help them find more money.

Much of their rush-to-patent frenzy was motivated by determination to be first to market, which meant protecting their IP and "novel" idea as the forerunner, which is not an unusual start-up strategy. They were also operating under the false notion that patents, and more patents, equaled more product value, and that investors would flock to capitalize on this low-hanging moneymaker. Finally, the worst reason of all, owning a slew of patents made them feel like smart and savvy business owners.

When the time came to pitch the prototype to potential investors, the list of IP was impressive for sure, but could not overcome the fact that management had not spent the first round of investor money wisely. There wasn't an investor in sight who thought this particular team could lead the company through the rugged hills and valleys of acquiring more than a dozen patents, marketing the product, driving sales, producing endless iterations of the device, and, heaven forbid, making anything remotely resembling an IPO.

The outcome of this debacle was that the company burned through a ton of cash and never got high enough off the ground to have any kind of presence in the marketplace.

It's not advisable to rush into getting a patent, because filing for one can be expensive. Additionally, once you have filed for a patent, your idea is no longer a secret.

Patent-rich may mean cash-flow poor. Do your homework and make sure you absolutely need to get a patent. You will be better positioned to create maximum commercial value when the necessary and precautionary steps are taken to secure the concept if you do need IP protection.

Things you need to know if you are thinking of filing:

- How much prior art has been completed and who does it belong to?
- Can your technology be implemented into something else so infringement on your patent is hard to detect?
- If your invention has/will have global impact or applications, do you know how to file for international patents?
- Do you have the finances and constitution to litigate if you need to defend your patent?

Unless you are a knowledgeable patent attorney who can complete the needed tasks, it is advisable to find one to counsel and help you to legally and properly complete the IP process. This attorney assistance includes researching existing and/or potential competition, as well as patent defense mitigation. I strongly recommend you seek the services of a professional patent attorney if the decision is made to file for a patent. Attorneys should be found by referral only and always have references.

IF YOU ARE CONSIDERING A PATENT

Protection of IP is essential to your project if you are developing something as complicated as a new medical device. In return, IP stimulates medical advances, economic growth, and the introduction of new medical device developments.

Under U.S. patent law, an invention is patentable only if it meets the following four requirements:

- The invention must be patent-eligible subject matter
- The invention must be novel (original)
- The invention must be useful or have some utility
- The invention must be non-obvious

A patent is not used to protect an abstract idea. Instead, the idea must encapsulate at least one of the following patent-eligible subject matter categories:

- A novel and useful composition of matter
  (for example a new pharmaceutical)

- An article of manufacture
- A machine (for example having moving parts or circuitry)
- A process or method that is new or improved

Even within the above categories, there are inventions and discoveries that cannot be patented, for example mathematical formulas, capacities of the human body such as a new way to kick a football, substances that occur naturally in the earth, and ideas encompassing laws of nature.

Without specialized expertise, it may be difficult to assess the patentability of your invention, particularly because novelty and non-obviousness are assessed against what is already in the public domain, i.e., the prior art. So, if you do not have the expertise, you are well advised to seek the advice of a patent attorney or other patent expert that can assess patentability through a patent or novelty search and study.

Having a patent does not necessarily make you the owner of the invention, either. This is especially true if you have conceived your idea under the umbrella of a university or in a corporate setting. Become familiar with technology transfer policies if you find yourself in either of these environments.

It is also advisable to perform a clearance, or right-to-use, search and study of existing issued patents to make sure you are not inadvertently infringing on someone else's patent by making, using, or selling your new invention. It is possible to infringe another's patent by selling your invention even if your invention is patentable.

You might be surprised to note that ownership of a patent does not give you the right to make, use, and sell your invention. Rather, *it gives you the right to exclude others from making, using, and selling your claimed invention*. If there is a blocking patent, you may want to seek a license under that patent or consider design-arounds to avoid infringement. Again, you will likely need a patent attorney to perform these studies.

From a profit standpoint, even if the scientific merit or quality of the idea is sound, the big question is can you create value through commercialization?

Things to consider:

- Is your idea critical or timely?
- Is your idea a core or stand-alone technology?
- Will you need to jump through the many FDA hoops for approval? (i.e., for drugs and medical devices) in addition to your patent work?
- Do you have a prototype? Does it work?
- What additional applications does your invention have and how can you tap into these additional revenue sources?

ADVICE FROM INDUSTRY EXPERTS

What is the Best Way to Assess IP Value?

Terry Ludlow of Ontario, Canada, is a recognized leader and pioneer in the use of advanced electronics and semiconductor reverse engineering processes to support innovative product design and to extract maximum value from Intellectual Property (IP). He answers this question as follows:[17]

Patents can hold potential value in a wide range of business transactions. For example, a portfolio may be licensed or sold. A company may identify a new opportunity or use for an existing patent as technology evolves. This is especially true right now with the Internet of Things (IoT) where we see converging technologies giving rise to new use cases. Patent value should be a factor in any merger or acquisition, or when seeking additional investments. This begs the question, "What is the best way to assess the potential value or use of a patent portfolio?"

Before we examine this, it's important to clarify that a patent only has value in the context of its place in a portfolio and in how the portfolio is used to support the organization's business strategy. Let's look at two examples. A Patent Assertion Entity will evaluate patent value based solely on the potential revenue that will come from a licensing program. On the other hand, an operating company typically places a higher value on patents that provide protection. This can be the ability to defend leadership in a profitable market category or the ability to offer protection as a sole-sourced product's revenue stream.

In any case, the concepts presented here are intended only to offer guidance to companies actively transacting or licensing patents.

The traditional patent valuation techniques, cost, citation, market, and income-based, are not particularly relevant to IP and licensing professionals. Since they have no bearing on the true value of patents from a strategic business perspective, they will not be discussed in this section. Instead, we'll focus on the three essential factors that affect patent value:

1. *Patent validity*. This has to do with how claims were written, their ability to stand up to scrutiny under current legal systems, and whether or not they were truly new or could be subject to prior use assertions. Essentially, a consideration of whether the patent is valid.

2. *Technical merit*. This involves the usefulness of a patent's claimed invention, including its unique ability to solve a problem or be used in a particular product/product type. It is important to consider here whether or not the claims accurately reflect the invention.

3. *Market merit*. Essentially, this refers to how widely the invention protected by the patent is used in various products and markets. It takes into account its competitive position and the revenue it generates. It also examines whether or not the invention is part of an industry standard.

The Five-Step Patent Evaluation Process[18]

Terry Ludlow's Five-Step Evaluation Process helps entrepreneurs identify patents with high potential value and use.

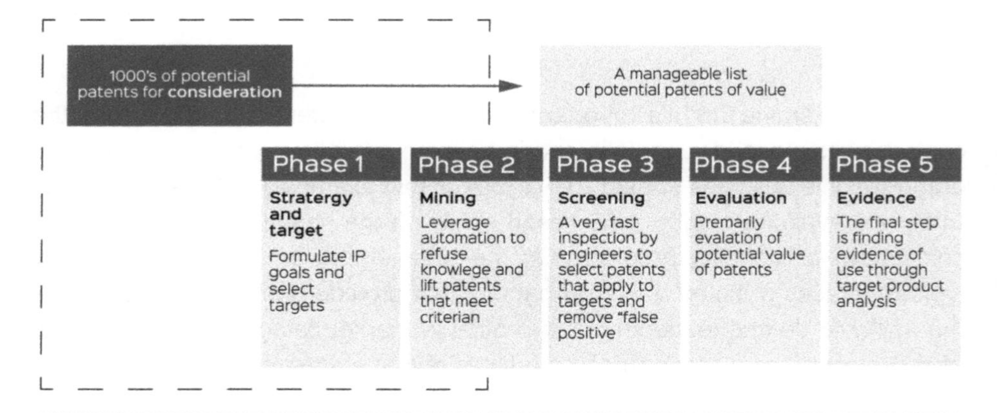

These five steps are explained as follows:

1. Identify targets that support your strategic business goals.

Patent brokers and Patent Assertion Entities (PAEs) consider who is using the patented technology, and whether the technology generates profits, reduces costs, and differentiates their potential licensee's products. They research how much revenue the products generate and how much the patented technology contributes to that profit. Typically, a PAE will only be interested if a licensing program has the potential to generate more income than it will cost.

Corporations also are interested in evaluating the potential for cross-licensing deals that provide access to new technology. This may generate new products and revenue for both parties. They are most interested in information on competitive advantages, revenue, and profit margin protection.

Regardless, focusing on specific targets with clear licensing objectives will better target the patent mining process and limit costs.

2. Complete patent mining to assess value.

While Subject Matter Experts (SMEs) are the best source for reading, analyzing, and mapping each patent and its claims, this approach can be time-consuming and cost-prohibitive, and hybrid approaches may be preferred. Today, sophisticated software allows patent mining to be completed prior to hands-on screening and analysis by SMEs. This pre-screening reduces the number of patents to assess and ensures that they have a high probability of value vis-à-vis the current program. Often, preliminary research and product reverse engineering — from teardown to semiconductor cross-sections — is required to further focus patent mining.

Patent mining should use a combination of keyword, classification code, and semantic language search as well as machine learning. Keyword searches require a good dictionary that includes synonyms, hypernyms, and hyponyms.

Classification code searches generally are useful only in the first phases of mining, as critical flaws equate to poor precision (relevance of patents kept) and recall (relevant patents missed). Semantic language searches enable a more-like-this search paradigm, which lessens the need for controlled technical dictionaries.

Finally, machine learning trains algorithms to find patents in a portfolio based on example patents that represent the technology concept.

Patent topographic maps automatically render text-based technology clusters, which are used to find patents on technologies more likely to be used in target products, and to identify white space or gaps in a portfolio. Good mapping tools provide flexible color overlays and include machine learning algorithms and Boolean search to turn patents (dots) on / off. The most valuable topographic map strikes an optimal balance between detail and trend analysis and conveys strategic information to all IP stakeholders. These tools should overlay lists of "proud" or "star" patents, competitors' patents, date ranges, IPCs, existing hits, or any other patent metadata on a portfolio map to yield insights.

Remember, patent mining is inherently difficult, and outliers can be missed. Therefore, don't automatically abandon patents that were not identified for further study.

3. Screen for relevant patents.

SMEs should complete a quick review of the patents that the software tools produced. This helps refine the list of relevant patents and eliminates false positives, patents that may have been selected but don't support the objectives or read on the target. This screening also identifies outliers or false negatives that have potential value. Recovering these requires further iterative mining steps with different parameters.

Screening is especially important if the first analysis failed to generate the desired number of potentially infringed patents. After screening, the patents are divided by subject and by some basic measure of value, e.g., high/medium/low rankings. This process is often assisted by text mining, which allows you to direct smaller piles of patents to the correct SME for detailed evaluation.

4. Evaluate.

During the evaluation process, the SMEs read and analyze the claims. A multi-part rating system can be applied to rate

- the probability of use in industry
- the ease of proof of the claims
- the perceived risk of prior art/prior use being found

Identifying patents at risk allows analysts the opportunity to either eliminate a patent with prior art exposure or to better understand the claim limitations and improve the quality and enforceability of claims. A high-priority patent is used in the industry and can be documented easily, while a medium-priority patent is more expensive and difficult to document. Remember, all of the ratings are opinions based on the reviewers' experience and quickly sourced references.

5. Map your product and search for evidence.

Evidence of use is the cornerstone of most IP licensing and transaction negotiations. Without proof, these negotiations often fail. The most compelling evidence of use is accurate and detailed claim charts. These offer concrete proof that a patented invention is being used in a product, and show how the claims are being interpreted. Today, the most powerful claim charts often are developed using sophisticated instruments, complex analytical techniques, and highly skilled SMEs.

A patent-to-product matrix is developed that reflects the program objectives and the patent evaluation. The matrix maps high-probability patents to products already being manufactured by potential licensing targets. Both the patents and the products can be segmented by a number of criteria that are used to assess potential risk, damages, and royalty fees. These criteria include the patent rating, the market or current and forecasted future sales volume, and the product revenue.

The patent-product matrix is an important tool. It demonstrates how effectively a patent portfolio covers a potential licensing partner's product line and revenue. Using a standard damages model and royalty rates you can calculate the potential and cumulative value of your patents. The first patent covering a specific product and technology is always the most valuable. Subsequent patents covering the same products and technology diminish in value exponentially as the number of patents in this cluster grows.

THE TAKEAWAY

The most effective way to identify valuable patents in any portfolio is to rely on a combination of proven processes, advanced tools, and experienced SMEs. Knowledge of the richness of your portfolio optimizes your licensing opportunities and enables the formation of a more effective patent and IP strategy.

Help! My IP Is Being Used Without Permission!

Once you understand how the patent and IP process works, your next question may be, "What should I do if I find my intellectual property being used without permission?"

It is easier than ever to be inspired by others' work or products online in today's digital world. It is easier still to take that work or product and attempt to re-create and pass it off as your property.

Finding out that the idea you worked so hard to bring from brain to bank has been stolen and sold by someone else can be heartbreaking or rage-inducing, depending on the circumstances.

Either way, you may be tempted to rush in and punish those who are using your IP with litigation and other punitive measures. However, before you rush to judgment, asking yourself a few questions (after a deep breath) can help you avoid expensive court costs and a potential loss of time, energy, and resources.

Questions to Ask Before You Move Ahead with IP Litigation

"Have I Properly Protected My Intellectual Property?"

The first question you must ask yourself is whether or not you have taken the proper steps to protect your intellectual property from being used without your consent or permission.

If your product or idea hasn't been protected with the proper patents or IP legal protections, you may not have the legal standing to sue or demand that the perpetrator stop.

"Did They Come Up with This Idea Before I Did?"

Sometimes another product or design may look like your own idea but was created and brought to the market before yours. This is unfortunate — but not uncommon. Sometimes you just get beaten to the punch in the competitive marketplace.

"Would It Be Better to Just Ask Nicely?"

The best action may be to simply request in a well-worded letter that the offender "cease and desist" from using your intellectual property.

You may be shocked to find that some individuals simply didn't realize that what they were doing was wrong, and will immediately comply with a nice but firm request that they stop using and selling your IP.

"Am I Ready for The Legal Costs and Process?"

Suppose you've exhausted all of your options and resources and the other party simply refuses to stop using your intellectual property. In that case, it may be time to take the situation to the next level.

However, before you move forward with potential legal action, you will need to ensure you are ready to handle the court costs and fees associated with IP legal cases.

Working closely with a trusted legal advisor, you can get a better idea of what costs and resources may be required of you to bring your case to court. An advisor will also be able to show you how to get the most out of your case to cover any potential damages.

Expect The Best, Prepare for The Worst

When it comes to IP, knowing how to handle potential legal issues is essential. You don't want to go off-course while bringing your idea to market by getting caught up in endless legal battles.

While you should never allow yourself or your business to be taken advantage of, expecting the best outcome will help you avoid headaches and heartache. At the same time, preparing yourself for the worst by obtaining the right protections for your idea can help you avoid potential pitfalls down the road.

CHAPTER 9 - Action Accelerators

THINK IT → ORGANIZE IT → DO IT

Take action on these items NOW to keep driving your idea from Brain to Bank:

1. Determine if you truly need to patent your invention:
    - The invention must be patent-eligible subject matter
    - The invention must be original
    - The invention must be useful or have some utility
    - The invention must not be obvious

2. If you can affirm you meet the criteria above, the next step is to determine whether your idea is encapsulated in one of these patent eligible subject matter categories:
    - A composition of matter (for example, a new pharmaceutical)
    - An article of manufacture
    - A machine (for example, having moving parts or circuitry)
    - A process or method

3. Assess the potential value or use of your patent portfolio with The Five-Step Patent Evaluation Process.

4. Seek out a reputable patent attorney by getting referrals and references. Connect with him/her and take advantage of a free first consultation to see if you truly need a patent.

5. Update your roadmap so it has the most current information.

STICK TO THE PLAN

Chapter 10

Show Me the Money

NOTE: This chapter is more advanced. Please consult the glossary in the back of the book when needed to ward off panic attacks of inadequacy or paralyzing confusion.

MONEY 101

We all know there are 50 ways to leave your lover, but did you know there are more than 100 names for money?[19] Let's start with slang references to edibles, and then branch out from there:

1. bananas
2. bread
3. dough
4. roll
5. cabbage
6. lettuce
7. kale
8. bacon
9. clams
10. coconuts
11. beans
12. fish
13. potatoes
14. chips
15. buckaroos
16. bucks
17. fins ($5-bills)
18. sawbucks ($10-bills)
19. C-notes ($100-bills)
20. hundies
21. dead presidents
22. Benjamins
23. Franklins
24. Jacksons
25. grand
26. Gs
27. K
28. smack
29. smackers
30. wampum
31. bills
32. moolah
33. means
34. checks
35. drafts
36. shrapnel
37. wad
38. plaster
39. bankroll
40. capital
41. finances
42. currency
43. funds
44. gold
45. stash
46. cash
47. bundle
48. fortune
49. lucre
50. chump change
51. pin money
52. shekels
53. resources
54. boffo
55. fiat
56. doubloons
57. wherewithal
58. treasure
59. dibs
60. bits
61. dollars
62. dinero
63. pesos
64. bullets
65. coin
66. simoleons
67. silver
68. pelf
69. tender
70. scrip
71. pittance
72. guineas
73. gelt
74. bones
75. stake
76. pap
77. spondulicks
78. quid
79. specie
80. jack
81. change
82. scratch
83. wonga
84. king's ransom
85. mint
86. paper
87. loonies
88. mazuma
89. pieces of eight
90. frogskins
91. long green
92. folding green
93. green
94. greenbacks
95. riches
96. rivets
97. big ones
98. banknotes
99. chits
100. scrilla
101. loot
102. do-re-mi

Call it what you like... moolah, capital, or a pain in the buck... when you're creating a new service or product, finding money is almost always one of the first problems that arises.

The good news is there are many investment streams you can navigate, including family and friends, angels, venture capital, private placement, crowdfunding, and others.

As a disclaimer, please know that raising capital is a highly regulated activity. The purpose of the following section is to provide you with information on this topic, and nothing here should be construed as creating, offering, or memorializing the existence of an attorney-client relationship. The content should not be considered legal advice or opinion, because the content may not apply to the specific facts of a particular matter or you or your project or your company. Alpha 81 does not provide investment advice, endorse any products, or endorse companies that offer investment opportunities. All information and materials are for educational purposes only. All parties are strongly encouraged to consult with their attorneys, accountants, and financial advisors before entering into any type of investment.

ADVICE FROM INDUSTRY EXPERTS

Now, to answer some of your unasked questions. The information below[20] comes from a presentation given by Brian Burt, a brilliant, seasoned, Harvard Law School–educated corporate attorney with the Snell & Wilmer law firm:

Who provides a new business with its initial capital?

The founder(s).

Who provides a business with its next round of capital?

The founder(s) and/or their family and friends. Yes, the first couple of go-arounds are on you... you the founder, you the entrepreneur, and yes, you the bank. Only after there is sufficient skin in the game — your skin — and progress on a prototype and initial sales will most other types of investors think about coming on board.

Identify Sources of Capital

Here are some of the investment capital avenues available:

- Founders
- Friends and family
- Angel investors (individual or organized groups), who need proof of concept
- Venture capital
- Strategic investors (customers, suppliers, competitors)
- Foundations /incubator and accelerator programs
- Commercial banks
- Commercial finance companies
- Asset-based lending, factoring
- Merchant banks
- Government (e.g., SBA loan, Small Business Innovation Research (SBIR) Small Business Technology Transfer Research (STTR) grants, E-5 Visa
- Initial Public Offering
- Employee Stock Ownership Plan (ESOP)
- Franchising
- Self-directed IRAs

How Much is Enough?

Determining your capital requirements is a tricky exercise. For example:

How much capital do you need?

- Enough to achieve the next significant company milestone (...but plan for the unexpected)
- Enough to get off the fundraising trail so you can focus on the business
- An amount that will not cause excessive dilution[21]

Do I need more than cash (i.e., "smart money")? Yes, you need:

- General business or industry expertise
- Access to investors' networks
- Strategic relationships

Can those needs be met without selling equity? Yes, you can consider a:

- Loan
- Grant
- Contractual relationship
- Joint venture ownership of a new company

CAPITALIZING YOUR COMPANY

The Funding Gap

Stage	Pre-Seed	Seed/ Start-Up		Early	Later
Source	Founders, Friends, and Family	Individual Angels	**Funding Gap between $500,000and $2,000,000/$5,000,000** (depending on region)	Venture Funds	
Investment	$25,000 to $100,000	$100,000 to $500,000		$2,000,000/$5,000,000 and up	

Source: Angel Capital Education Foundation

A funding gap refers to the difference between the amount of financing required to implement a project or program and the amount that is currently available. It can occur in government, nonprofit, or business contexts and represents the additional funds needed to reach a specific goal or complete a project successfully. The funding gap is often an obstacle that must be overcome through fundraising, grants, loans, or other forms of financing.

Comply with Security Laws

Once you have exhausted your own money, you'll most likely need to expand into other avenues to keep your new company up and running. This is where things can get tricky, like complying with securities laws and such.

Knowing what a security is, and is not, is important. According to the Securities Act of 1933 – Section 2(a)(1):

Any note, stock, treasury stock, security future, bond, debenture, evidence of indebtedness, certificate of interest or participation in any profit-sharing agreement, collateral-trust certificate, pre-organization certificate or subscription, transferable share, investment contract, voting-trust certificate, certificate of deposit for a security, fractional undivided interest in oil, gas, or other mineral rights, any put, call, straddle, option, or privilege on any security, certificate of deposit, or group or index of securities (including any interest therein or based on the value thereof), or any put, call, straddle, option, or privilege entered into on a national securities exchange relating to foreign currency, or, in general, any interest or instrument commonly known as a "security", or any certificate of interest or participation in, temporary or interim certificate for, receipt for, guarantee of, or warrant or right to subscribe to or purchase, any of the foregoing.

Failure to comply with SEC regulations may:

- Cause the investment to be unwound (rescission rights)
- Impact your ability to raise capital in the future
- Impact or even prevent the ultimate sale of the company
- Impact your ability to finance future companies
- Result in civil and criminal penalties for the company and its principals

When are securities laws triggered?

When 1 share of stock (or unit) is **offered** to 1 person

What laws are triggered?

1) Federal
2) State in which the company is located
3) State(s) in which investor(s) is located; Do not assume uniformity.

According to Mr. Burt, there are many myths surrounding SEC exemptions you should ignore as well as transaction exemptions you can utilize:

Common Offering Exemption Myths

Myth #1 The "Good Deal" Exemption
Myth #2 The "Everyone Else Does It" Exemption
Myth #3 The "Only My Friends and Family Are Investing" Exemption
Myth #4 The "What I Don't Know Can't Hurt Me" Exemption
Myth #5 The "We Are Only Issuing Shares to 1 Person" Exemption
Myth #6 The "We Are Only Raising a Little Money" Exemption
Myth #7 The "Regulators Are Focused on The Big Guys" Exemption

The good news is that there are transaction exemptions for both Federal and State laws available based on:

- Number, financial sophistication, and location of investors, and their relation to the company (if any)
- Value of securities being issued
- Type of disclosure contemplated or desired

- Manner of soliciting participants contemplated or desired
- Plans for additional offerings in the near term

It's understandable to feel overwhelmed about this aspect of your project. Unless you went to law school, some (or all) of this is as foreign to you as an ability to speak Sentinelese just because you happen to get shipwrecked in North Sentinel Island, a small island in the Indian Ocean.

But you're not stranded, and there is a ship to save you on the horizon. You don't have to figure all of this out on your own; this is one of those times when DIY isn't your best option and a competent corporate attorney can rescue you. In the long run, you will pay less money for an attorney than you will for the mistakes you will make if you go it alone.

What It Means to Have Investors

When you bring on investors, it's no longer just your company. You have "roommates" now. Certain responsibilities and ramifications emerge:

Fiduciary duties

The board of directors has fiduciary duties to the company's stockholders.

Corporate protocols

The company must follow statutory and governing document requirements for officer appointments, board elections, and meetings, shareholder meetings, stock issuances, etc. The company is also subject to a shareholder's agreement.

Investor relations, which can impact future ventures

It's a small world and there may be another company you will want to start. Take care of your relationships with your investors.

The Investor Agreement

An important aspect of working with investors are the legal agreements between your investors and your company. I cannot stress enough the importance of using an attorney for contracts, and, if needed, for negotiations, to produce binding corporate agreements.

Another Episode in the Entrepreneurial Drama Series *I Didn't See It Coming*

I worked with a company that was developing a subdivision and building new, single-family housing. The founder needed cash, so he brought in a general contractor/investor partner.

The founder cut and pasted the Investor Agreement together from various documents he found on the internet and presented it to the contractor. Not wanting to spend money on an attorney, the contractor read the Agreement on his own and signed it. He was anxious to get started.

Only a month into the project, the contractor discovered that the founder was not just short on cash, but very short on cash, and couldn't put the agreed amount into the project. Having already invested a large sum of cash and with the first three homes under construction, the contractor felt not only lied to, but also compelled to keep the project going, lest he lose his own money. So, he put in more cash.

The contractor continued to dump more money into the project while the founder put in nothing, claiming he was waiting for the closing of another property, when he would have more money to put in.

The three new spec homes were well under way, and the contractor had subcontractors who relied on him to continue the project, finish it, and pay them. How could he not keep the project going?

The contractor partner dug deeper and deeper into his pockets until, without telling his wife, he took out a home equity loan on their own house and dumped that into the development kitty. He now had put in 85 percent of the invested equity.

The contractor then learned a shocking truth. The founder/partner had been lying to his own wife about the amount of money the contractor/investor had put in, saying he was merely the contractor and a small minority investor in the project. The founder told his wife he was the one who had put in the majority of the funds.

Does the movie *Dumb and Dumber* come to mind?

The contractor calls the founder's home. The wife will not let the contractor talk to her husband. The contractor explains what has been going on and the wife calls him a liar and hangs up.

The founder's wife immediately goes on a rampage and tells her husband she will take over from here. Out of the blue, this suburban housewife who has never worked a job in her life, let alone run a $10 million project, and who has spent most of her waking days watching *Days of Our Lives*, is now the contractor's new partner.

Yes, the agreement allowed the founder to give his partnership to whomever he liked whenever he liked without the consent of any partners.

I know, I know, you're thinking how utterly stupid the contractor was for not seeing this in the agreement. But the language was such that he simply didn't pick up on it. It was intentionally deceptive, but legal.

Many weeks and massive attorney fees later — not to mention a trip to the emergency room for bleeding ulcers; the contractor sold his equity in the project to the founder (funny how the founder now had the cash to buy him out), and the contractor broke even.

You're seeing the lesson in this one, right? Call Saul, or your own attorney, or a well-known corporate attorney recommended to you, and get someone on your team that has the smartz to read between the lines. The alternative is not pretty.

How To Find the Right Corporate Attorney

Hopefully, this chapter has made one fact crystal clear: when money and investors get involved, things can get convoluted quickly. Thankfully, there are trained professionals who make a living helping small business owners and entrepreneurs avoid the pitfalls of legal issues and financial problems. Should you find yourself facing legal issues or confusing paperwork at any point in your journey, a corporate lawyer or business attorney may be one of your most valuable friends and partners.

If you are looking to invest in a long-term partnership, consider a corporate attorney for your business. Even more than a highly sought-after investor or VC, a skilled corporate attorney can be a lifesaver if things go wrong.

What Is a Corporate or Business Attorney?

A business or corporate attorney is just that — a skilled legal professional who is focused on helping companies succeed. However, business attorneys cover much more than simply court cases — they can step in and offer guidance and services for tons of the essential aspects of building your business:

- Corporate Organization
- Reorganization and Governance
- Private Equity and Debt Financing
- Securities Regulation
- Shareholder/Owner Relations
- Joint Ventures and Strategic Alliances
- Writing and Preparing Business Plans
- Employment and Consulting Agreements
- Employee Incentive Programs
- General Contract Negotiation
- Supplier/Manufacturing Agreements
- Technology Transfer and Licensing
- Fund Formation
- Corporate Asset Protection
- Exit Strategy and Succession Planning
- Mergers And Acquisitions
- Buyouts And Disputes

Your business attorney will have the expertise and experience to walk you through a variety of aspects of starting and managing your business — and is often your go-to individual to help you navigate the tight turns of a new venture and keep you on the right track.

5 Steps to Selecting the Right Corporate Attorney

1. **Remember Why a Business Attorney Is Essential to Success**

   Before you ever hire an attorney, you must know why you may want to hire one. Here's the good news: if you've read this far, then you have already completed step one.

   By knowing the potential legal and financial issues you might face along the way from mind to market, you will be better prepared to find the right attorney for you.

2. **Ask Other Entrepreneurs**

   I always ask other entrepreneurs whom they use for their corporate attorney. It's like checking out how many reviews and gold stars are attached to a specific Amazon product and using this information to choose whether to buy it; we all know that 2,769 reviews averaging 4.5 stars can't all be wrong. In fact, it's reassurance that we, too, are making a smart choice.

3. **Check Out Local or Online Attorney Services**

   If you are ready to start looking for a competent corporate attorney, you can start by checking out the local offerings in your city.

   You can also take advantage of online business attorney services through resources such as LegalZoom or Rocket Lawyer. Many of these sites offer legal services and can help you incorporate your business — and they fit into many early-stage budgets. Again… read the reviews.

4. **Compare Your Potential Attorneys with the Right Questions**

   Don't pick the first attorney you find in your city or online. Make sure you come to the table with the right questions and make sure they offer the unique services you need to build your business and handle issues that you may run into in the days ahead.

5. **Interview Potential Attorneys**

   It's imperative to interview the attorneys you are considering — ideally in person, but at least via webcam — to gauge their grasp of what you need and their ability to provide it. Also, you'll get a better sense of "fit" and of whether you'll be able to work with him/her to accomplish your legal goals.

6. Invest - But Don't Bust Your Budget

The final step is to work out a retainer fee for having your business attorney work as a partner in taking your idea from concept to cash. Remember that getting legal guidance and protection is an investment in both your idea and your future, but don't bust your current budget for services you may not need at the moment. Keep space available for adding extra legal help, should the time come.

CHAPTER 10 - Action Accelerators

THINK IT → ORGANIZE IT → DO IT

Take action on these items NOW to keep driving your idea from Brain to Bank:

1. Determine if, and how, your company can make money.

2. Make every dollar count. Write down how you will do this.

3. Determine your capital requirements and set realistic funding/timing expectations.

4. Prepare to sell your investment opportunity (i.e., tell your story) with real pro formas. You can easily do the pro formas in LivePlan if you didn't complete them in Chapter 5.

5. Practice your pitch on friends and family… who knows, maybe they will buck up right then and there!

6. Hire an attorney to answer questions and get you through the tough parts of legally raising capital and bringing on investors.

7. Update your roadmap so it has the most current information.

STICK TO THE PLAN

Chapter 11
Design for Manufacturability

NOTE: This chapter is more advanced. Please consult the glossary in the back of the book when needed to ward off panic attacks of inadequacy or paralyzing confusion.

OPTIMIZING AND REFINING YOUR PRODUCT DESIGN

Paramount in creating a successful end product is working closely with the manufacturer in the design phase. This collaboration builds value into the product. For example, if design changes can be made to increase production efficiency while meeting the end-use requirements, it's a win-win for all involved. At the end of the day, the product needs to be manufactured in a cost-effective manner, so design with that end in mind.

Another Episode in the Entrepreneur Drama Series
I Didn't See It Coming

I have consulted with hundreds of companies over the years. This company's blatant disregard for expert advice and the Design for Manufacturability (DFM) protocols of a successful and experienced manufacturer tops them all.

A medical device company had designed a high-pressure molding for injection syringes. Even though it was potentially a multi-million-dollar tool deal, the company chose not to work with their manufacturer's engineers to make sure the device was both effective and cost-effective. Instead, they designed it on their own and then tried to force the manufacturer to produce it their way.

The manufacturer kept telling them their design wouldn't work. The medical device company's VP of Operations insisted it would. Feeling railroaded into abandoning its own well-proven DFM protocol, the manufacturer sent over a waiver to be signed indicating that if the end product did not work the manufacturer was not responsible. Once again, the medical company's VP insisted he was right, and willingly signed the wavier.

The end result proved the manufacturer was right about everything. The medical company ended up with boxes of product that could possibly be used as boat anchors, but never as syringe molds. It was a total failure in every way.

Just take a second and do the math on what is not working within the DFM protocol cost that medical device company: $2.5 million in useless tools, 18 months of lost time in production, and $13 million lost in contracts with customers depending on the delivery of those tools. Ego has its price.

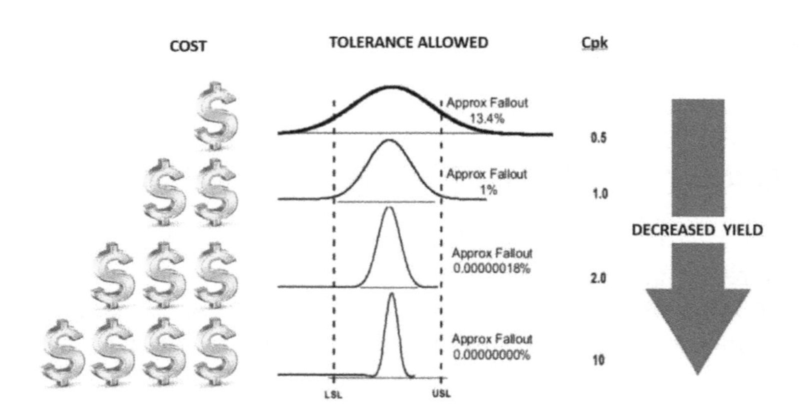

ADVICE FROM INDUSTRY EXPERTS

What is Design for Manufacturing or DFM?

I have an excellent partner in manufacturing I collaborate with whenever I really need things done right. Which, of course, is always. East West Manufacturing is a global manufacturing company able to manage projects from design to delivery.

This is their expert view and explanation of designing for manufacturability:

Design for Manufacturing (DFM) is the process of designing parts, components, or products for ease of manufacturing with an end goal of making a better product at a lower cost. This is done by simplifying, optimizing, and refining the product design. The acronym DFMA (Design for Manufacturing and Assembly) is sometimes used interchangeably with DFM.

Five principles are examined during a DFM. They are:

1. Process
2. Design
3. Material
4. Environment
5. Compliance/Testing

Ideally, DFM needs to occur early in the design process, well before tooling has begun. In addition, properly executed DFM needs to include all the stakeholders — engineers, designers, contract manufacturers, mold builders, and material suppliers. The intent of this "cross-functional" DFM is to challenge the design — to look at the design at all levels: component, sub-system, system, and holistic levels — to ensure the design is optimized and does not have unnecessary cost embedded in it.

The following chart offers an excellent visual representation of the effect of an early DFM. As the design progresses through the product life cycle, changes become more expensive, as well as more difficult to implement. Early DFM allows design changes to be executed quickly, at the least expensive location.

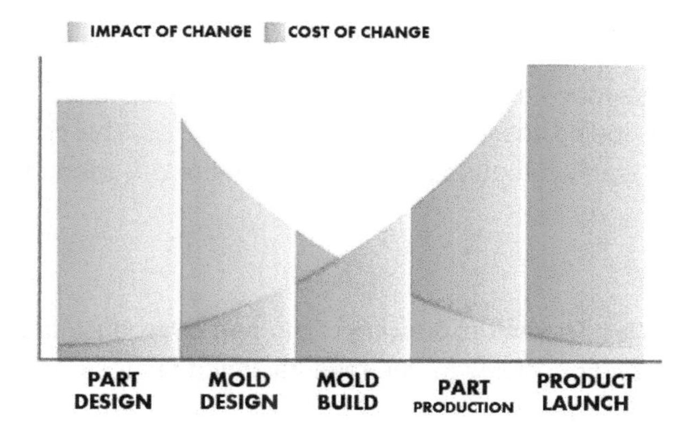

Pulling stakeholders together early in the design process is easier if you're developing a new product, but even if you're dealing with an established product, challenging the original design is a necessary element of a thorough DFM.

Too often, mistakes in a design are repeated by replicating a previous design or design element. Be sure to question every aspect of your design.

- Look at the original drawings.
- Tear down the product.

- Look at competitive and near-neighbor products, as well as lead users such as medical and automotive.
- Talk to your contract manufacturer who may have solved the problem with a different customer.
- Has someone else solved this problem in a different way.
- Is there a way to make it better?

A lot of thought, time, and effort go into a DFM. But in the end, you'll get a much better, more cost-effective product.

5 PRINCIPLES OF DFM: A CLOSER LOOK

1 Process

The manufacturing process chosen must be the correct one for the part or product. You wouldn't want to use a highly capitalized process like injection molding, which involves the building of tools and dies to make a low-volume part that could have been manufactured using a less capitalized method, such as thermoforming. This would be equivalent to using a tank to squash an anthill — a classic case of overkill.

In determining the manufacturing process, the DFM takes into consideration the quantity of parts being made, the material being used, the complexity of the surfaces, the tolerances required, and whether there are secondary processes required.

2 Design

Design is essential. The actual drawing of the part or product has to conform to good manufacturing principles for the manufacturing process you've chosen.

For example, in the case of plastic injection molding, the following principles would apply:

- Constant wall thickness, which allows for consistent and quick part cooling
- Appropriate draft (1 - 2 degrees is usually acceptable)
- Texture — 1 degree for every 0.001" of texture depth on texture sidewalls
- Ribs — 60 percent of the nominal wall, as a rule of thumb
- Simple transitions from thick to thin features
- Wall thickness not too small — this increases injection pressure

- No undercuts or features that require side action — all features "in line of pull/mold opening"
- Spec the loosest tolerances that allow a good product, and consult the trade organization for your manufacturing process on what is reasonable for that process

Be sure to discuss the design with your contract manufacturer, who can ensure your design conforms to good manufacturing principles for the selected process.

3 Material

It's important to select the correct material for your part/product.
Some material properties to consider during DFM include:

- Mechanical properties — How strong does the material need to be?
- Optical properties — Does the material need to be reflective or transparent?
- Thermal properties — How heat-resistant does it need to be?
- Color — What color does the part need to be?
- Electrical properties — Does the material need to act as a dielectric (that is, as an insulator rather than a conductor)?
- Flammability — How flame/burn resistant does the material need to be?

Again, be sure to discuss the material with your contract manufacturer, who might have access to existing materials in their portfolio which would allow you to secure lower material pricing.

4 Environment

Your part/product must be designed to withstand the environment it will be subjected to. All the form in the world won't matter if the part can't function properly under its normal operating conditions.

5 Compliance/Testing

All products must comply with safety and quality standards. Some of these are industry standards, others are third-party standards, and some are internal, company-specific standards.

Your manufacturer should have ISO-certified testing facilities. Find out who will provide UL (Underwriters Laboratory), ETL (Electrical Testing Labs), and other third-party testing. Where will that testing take place?

FACTORS THAT AFFECT DFM

The goal of DFM is to reduce manufacturing costs without reducing performance. In addition to the principles of DFM, here are seven actions that can improve your design for manufacturing and design for assembly:

1 Minimize Part Count

Reducing the number of parts in a product is the quickest way to reduce cost, because you are reducing the amount of material required, the amount of engineering, production, labor, all the way down to shipping costs.

2 Standardize Parts and Materials

Personalization and customization are expensive and time-consuming. Using quality standardized parts can shorten time to production, as such parts are typically available, and you can be more certain of their consistency. Material is based on the planned use of the product and its function. Consider:

- How should it feel? Hard? Soft?
- Does it need to withstand pressure?
- Will your part or product need to conduct heat, electricity?

3 Create Modular Assemblies

Using non-customized modules/modular assemblies in your design allows you to modify the product without losing its overall functionality. A simple example is a basic automobile that allows you to add in extras by putting in a modular upgrade.

4 Design for Efficient Joining

Can the parts interlock or clip together? Look for ways to join parts without the use of screws, fasteners, or adhesives. If you must use fasteners, here are a few tips:

- Keep the number, size, and variation of fasteners to a minimum
- Use standard fasteners as much as possible.
- Use self-tapping and chamfered screws for better placement.
- Stay away from screws too long or too short, separate washers, tapped holes, round heads, and flatheads.

5 Minimize Reorientation of Parts During Assembly & Machining

Parts should be designed so only a minimum of manual interaction is necessary during production and assembly.

6 Streamline Number of Manufacturing Operations/Processes

The more complex the process of making your product, the more possibilities for error are introduced. Remember that all processes have limitations and capabilities. Only include those operations essential to the function of the design.

7 Define "Acceptable" Surface Finishes

Unless it must be trade show grade, go with function rather than flashy for your surface finish.

10 OUTCOMES OF AN EFFECTIVE DFM

The book *Computer-Aided Manufacturing* offers 10 generally accepted Design for Manufacturing principles that were developed to help designers decrease the cost and complexity of manufacturing a product. The results of a successful DFM are quantifiable in a host of ways.

1. *Minimize the number of product parts.* Limiting the number of parts in your product is an easy way to lower the cost of a product. Why? Because it automatically reduces the amount of material and assembly labor required. Reducing the number of parts also means less engineering, production, labor, and shipping costs.
2. *Use standardized parts wherever possible.* Customization is not only expensive, it's time-consuming. Standardized parts are already made to meet the same quality metrics, every time. They are already tooled. So you save money and you won't have to wonder whether the parts will pass inspection.
3. *Create a modular design.* Using modules can simplify any future product redesign, and it also allows for use of standard components and the re-use of modules in other projects.
4. *Design multi-functional parts.* This seems rather obvious, but it's a simple way to reduce the total number of parts: design parts with more than one function.
5. *Design multi-use products.* Building on the point above, different products can share parts that have been designed for multi-use. Can your product use standardized parts that can be used in multiple products?
6. *Design for ease of fabrication.* Choose the ideal combination of material and manufacturing process that will minimize production costs. Ridiculously tight tolerances are a no-no. Avoid expensive and labor-extensive final operations like painting, polishing, and finish machining.

7. *Design your product to join without using screws, fasteners, or adhesives.* Is it possible for your product to interlock or clip together? Screws add only about 5 percent to the material cost, but 75 percent to the assembly labor. Remember: if fasteners are required, try to keep the size, number, and type to a minimum and use standard fasteners whenever possible.
8. *Design your part to minimize handling, especially during production and assembly.* Handling includes positioning, orienting, and fastening the part into place. For orientation purposes, use symmetrical parts wherever possible.
9. *Minimize assembly direction.* If possible, your parts should assemble from one direction. Ideally, parts should be added from above, parallel to the gravitational direction (a.k.a. downward). This way, assembly is facilitated by gravity rather than fought by it.
10. *Design your part to maximize compliance.* Rely on built-in design features like tapers or chamfers, or moderate radius sizes, to guide the insertion of equipment and to protect the part from damage.

It's been said that about 70 percent of the manufacturing costs of a product — the cost of materials, processing, and assembly — are determined by design decisions. If that's the case, then you want to make sure you are adhering to the best design practices possible.

HOW LONG WILL THE DFM TAKE?

You might be wondering what kind of time you'll have to invest in the DFM. That depends on the quality of the design that you start with.

One of my engineers likened it to proofreading an essay. For example, if you understand the writer's intent, it's much easier to make the corrections in the text. But if you're reading the essay without a clear understanding of intent, you might go back and forth with corrections before you come up with a finished copy.

The DFM is similar. Perhaps the design is clean, answering all questions for all parties. You'll be ready to go in a day or two. But depending on the number of questions, their difficulty, and the speed and thoroughness of the answers, you might be waiting a week or more. Take a deep breath. Your contract manufacturer will be able to give you a better idea of how long they think it will take. Remember speed isn't the goal: a quality product is.

A good DFM hopefully concludes by reducing the complexity of the design and satisfying the customer's requirements for price, specification, material, and scheduling.

In other words, the design is deemed manufacturable and ready for the next step on the road to production.

Don't Get Lost in the DFM Weeds

As you've read, the DFM process is an essential part of the design and manufacturing process and trying to skip steps or build your own shortcut can lead to disastrous results.

While following through the five stages of DFM, don't forget to keep your team, investors, and early backers well informed of your process. It is at this step that a variety of issues could arise that force you back and forth from the drawing board to the manufacturing floor waaaaaaay too many times.

If you allow yourself as the owner of the company to be caught up in the weeds of design and manufacturing and push deadlines and delivery dates back, you may risk losing your first supporters. Here are a few tips for keeping your key stakeholders involved and aware of what is happening throughout the DFM process:

Stay In Constant Contact

Remember those early days when you were so excited about WHY you were taking your idea from brain to bank and you couldn't stop talking about it with others? Why stop now when you are truly designing for manufacturing?

Create simple and effective ways you can keep your key stakeholders involved throughout the DFM process with updates, behind-the-scenes information, and just enough content to keep their mouths watering for the final product. Oh... and lots of the enthusiasm that got you started in the first place!

Be Honest About Timelines

During DFM, things might come up which potentially force you to redream and redesign your product. Sometimes, these changes can lead to delays or changes in delivery dates. If you have created an expectation about when a prototype will be available to your team or investors — and an issue or change delays that deliverable — make sure you keep them updated with honest feedback on what's happening. More often than not, your investors will be thrilled that you are making the product better.

Celebrate Wins Creatively

The DFM process will often be focused on overcoming problems that only occur once you "get in the car, start the ignition, and head down the road." Don't forget to keep your eyes peeled for small wins that you can highlight along the way. This will help ease the burden of the design process and keep all parties engaged. For example, did you come across a less expensive material source that will save you money and potentially allow you to add an unexpected feature? If you are confident that new aspect can make it from the drawing board to the prototype, pump up the team by celebrating that huge win!

Want to Truly Overdeliver? Overcommunicate!

This is a tip which shouldn't shock most entrepreneurs or idea creators, yet so few do it.

Overcommunicate Before, During, and After the DFM Process

Never underestimate the power of clear and concise communication. As you move into the design process, you will be shocked at how fast time starts flowing — and how quickly you can start to lose yourself (and your team and early supporters) in the journey.

You are on an exciting road trip bringing your idea to the marketplace. Remember to keep everyone informed of your progress at every turn.

5 THINGS TO LOOK FOR IN A DFM PARTNER[22]

You have an amazing product idea. It is gorgeous. It could be a major success. But can it be manufactured? All too often, we see brilliant ideas that simply can't be produced in an efficient or affordable way. This is where design for manufacturing comes into the picture. Design for Manufacturing (DFM) is the method of designing for ease of manufacturing of the assortment of parts that will form the product after assembly. DFM is primarily concerned with reducing overall part production costs and minimizing the complexity of manufacturing operations. Below are five things you should look for in any prospective solution provider:

Capabilities That Align with Your Project

First, make sure a prospective DFM partner has the capabilities and experience to handle your project. This includes having an excellent product design engineering team in place and experience making similar products of the quality level you're seeking. But taking their word for it isn't enough—be sure to visit their facility to vet their capabilities yourself.

Sophisticated Software

A great engineering team is a good start, but their expertise should be supplemented by advanced software, including systems for flow simulation, FEA, and tooling analysis. Such software subjects your design to real-world conditions, so you aren't left to make assumptions about its performance.

Choosing a solution provider who works without such software will be a source of regret in the long run, because without it, your design cannot be adequately optimized for manufacturability.

Seasoned, Global Supply Chain

Your DFM partner should assist with more than just design services. To fully maximize opportunities and cost savings, the company should be expert in strategic sourcing and ensuring the product is manufactured in the best location and have an extensive network of professionals within its supply chain. In addition to providing valuable know-how, this also expands your options for sourcing, manufacturing, assembly, shipping, and warehousing. Not only is supply chain breadth important, so is verticality, especially for critical areas like tooling.

Tailored Process

While a certain degree of structure and standardization is necessary, customization and flexibility within the process are equally important. The perfect DFM partner should cater to your unique needs and allow you to decide your level of involvement, whether this means simply going through the guided motions from start to finish or jumping in at various stages throughout the process.

Ensuring your engineering team works hand-in-hand with your DFM partner's engineering team is crucial. Collaboration should be the main focus in order to achieve success.

Company Culture and Accessibility

Just because a company is capable of designing your product for manufacturing doesn't mean they're the right fit. Consider their culture and values. Are they transparent and honest? Can you visit them, their facilities, and their third-party partners? Will they visit you in person to sort through the details? What sets these people apart from other DFM providers? Dig into this! Hopefully, you'll be starting a long-lasting partnership, so covering your bases on this front is a must before taking the plunge into a full-on DFM romance.

Whether you're looking for a company strictly offering DFM services or you're seeking a full-service supply chain partner, set the bar high.
Make a list of what you're looking for and stick to it. Don't settle for less. There are experienced, professional, flexible companies out there just waiting for you to waltz their way.

FDA REGISTRATION, REGULATORY, AND COMPLIANCE

If your brainchild is a medical device, this segment of the process will end your project quickly if you do not dot all of your i's and cross all of your t's. It is ongoing throughout your device development and is an intricate part of every step you take. The first item the FDA looks for in a submission is how the product was developed. Did the developer follow a formal Design Control Process, and do they have evidence of compliance with the process? Generally, design controls for medical devices are part of a broader Quality Management System (QMS) for the developing company.

When the U.S. Food and Drug Administration (FDA) reviews your design control requirements, their investigator will evaluate the control process, not determine if the design is appropriate, safe, or effective. The challenges of incorporating the design and development process into your QMS can be daunting. Since a significant number of medical device recalls are due to design problems, it is advisable for design controls to be in place prior to approval of the system-level requirements document and after completion of the feasibility phase.

FDA Title 21

The international industry standard defining the QMS is ISO 13485, which outlines all the various procedures and processes a well-run company needs to produce a quality, high-reliability product.

A formal submission to the FDA is required to receive clearance to market and sell medical products in the United States. This submission involves a wide range of documents that are a natural product of the QMS and design control process, including the product development plan, formal product requirement specifications, software requirement specifications, hardware requirement specifications, and verification test procedures and reports. These are the primary elements of an FDA submission from a design standpoint.

CLINICAL TRIALS/STUDIES PROJECT MANAGEMENT, EXECUTION, AND COMPLIANCE

Managing clinical trials of any size or complexity requires an expert in the field. This portion of the device development process will have five inherent stages: initiating, planning, executing, monitoring and controlling, and analysis and reporting.

Select a trial manager who knows how to include the details for developing and monitoring all aspects of the clinical trial, and also possesses the communication skills to keep you up to date.

To select a trial manager who will properly serve you and the specific clinical trial your device or product requires, research the following attributes:

1. Qualify the Contract Research Organization (CRO) by visiting the facility and checking out the range of expertise within the CRO. Hold meetings with management, scientists, and quality assurance personnel who would be involved in your trial.
2. Ensure the proposed CRO and selected professionals within that company are capable of doing the kind of work required (device vs. product vs. procedure) and that they work well as a team.
3. Conduct an investigators' meeting where all investigators and site staff are informed of the particularities of your clinical trial. During this meeting, be sure to provide background information for the clinical trial, why it is being conducted, and its clinical endpoints. This meeting is interactive and gives the participants a chance to ask questions.
4. Since the clinical trial must be supervised by a qualified person, confirm qualifications specific to your applicable regulations and guidelines.

CHAPTER 11 - Action Accelerators

THINK IT → ORGANIZE IT → DO IT

Take action on these items NOW to keep driving your idea from Brain to Bank:

1. How will you prepare to have the best outcome for the five areas examined during your DFM?

    1) Process

    ____

    2) Design

    ____

    3) Material

    ____

    4) Environment

    ____

    5) Compliance/Testing

    ____

2. Write down the five things to look for in a DFM partner:

    1) ______________________________

    2) ______________________________

    3) ______________________________

4) ______________________________

5) ______________________________

3. Update your roadmap so it has the most current information.

STICK TO THE PLAN

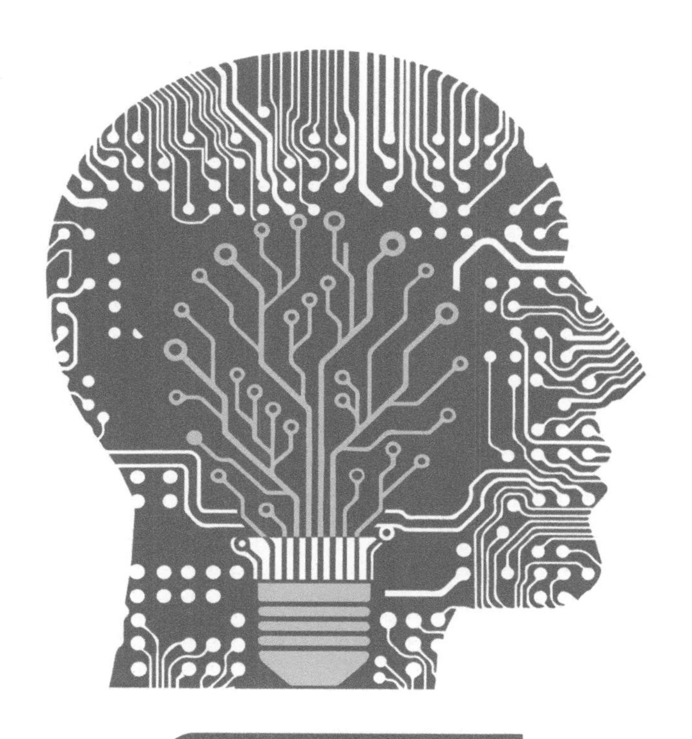

PART THREE

THE FINAL LAPS

Chapter 12
Your Ideal Customer

WHAT IS AN AVATAR?

In the past, when someone mentioned the word "avatar," all I could conjure up were images from James Cameron's blockbuster movie. In a 2007 interview with *Time* magazine, Cameron was asked about the meaning of the term *avatar*, to which he replied, "It's an incarnation of one of the Hindu gods taking a flesh form. In this film what that means is that the human technology in the future is capable of injecting a human's intelligence into a remotely located body, a biological body."

At the 82nd Academy Awards ceremony, Cameron's *Avatar* was nominated for nine Oscars, including for Best Picture and Best Director, and won three, for Best Art Direction, Best Cinematography, and Best Visual Effects. *Avatar* also garnered four nominations at the 67th Golden Globe Awards, and won for Best Motion Picture–Drama and Best Director.

The key reasons for the film's unprecedented success were its jaw-dropping visuals, excellent use of 3D, and the immersive setting of the lush jungle moon Pandora.

I know you're remembering what you learned about exponential technologies in Chapter 2, aren't you?

Although intriguing… I could go on and on about movies… let's focus on avatars. What does an avatar have to do with ideal customers?

An avatar in marketing is a profile of your ideal customer (or client). An avatar focuses on a particular type of person and goes into great detail about them. Customer avatar. Marketing persona. Buyer profile. Target market.

These are the terms spoken in marketing circles that represent the person most likely to buy your product or service.

It's a common mistake for business owners to focus on WHAT they're selling rather than WHO they are selling to. It doesn't matter if you have the most awesome product on earth if you're selling it to the wrong person.

This is why it is so important to discover your customer avatar from the start. You want to market to the right buyers.

Before you can effectively create the marketing aspect of your business plan, let alone sell your product or service, you need to understand:

- WHO is your ideal customer?
- WHERE are they hanging out online and in the real world?
- WHAT are their challenges?

Getting clear on who you are selling to is of paramount importance to all aspects of your business success. Understanding the demographics, interests, purchase drivers, fears, problems, challenges (often called pain points), and aspirations will help you create not only what others want, but also, most importantly, what they will buy.

This clarity begins with creating an avatar of your ideal customer.

ADVICE FROM INDUSTRY EXPERTS

Misty Kortes is a fellow Arizonan and colleague of mine. She is a passionate entrepreneur and business owner who has enabled many small companies to succeed when it comes to marketing their business. With her formal education in marketing, over two decades of speaking and training, and, more importantly, her real-life, in-the-trenches business experience, Misty now shares with you her insider secrets on creating the ideal customer avatar below:[23]

How to Create Your Customer Avatar

Buyer persona. Marketing persona. Customer avatar. Target market.

These are the phrases used interchangeably to describe the fictional, generalized representations of the buyer persona most likely to purchase from you.

It is critically important to the success of your marketing, sales, product development, and delivery of services that you have a deep understanding of who your customer avatar is. What is a customer avatar? You've likely heard the phrase, "You can't hit a target you haven't set." This applies perfectly to the importance of having a clearly defined customer avatar, which will help you:

- Determine which social platforms they are spending time on, so you know where your business should be present and active.
- Be more effective in your advertising. Your marketing dollars will be well spent when you know where to advertise and whom to target for maximum exposure.
- Write copy that connects with your marketing avatar, which will give you a better understanding of their pain points, goals, and successes.
- Deliver and develop better products and services, because you are able to anticipate your markets' needs, behaviors, and concerns.

So, having a clearly defined avatar is important; the question is, "How do I create one?" Good news: it's not difficult if you ask the right questions.

"What are the right questions?" you ask. You're in luck, because I've created a complete client avatar template to help out. This template makes it easy to compile all of your information, knowledge, experience, and research into one beautiful and presentable format.

Now, you could download the template I have created and begin filling it out right away, but the most effective client avatars are created with information based on market research as well as information that you gather from your current customer base.

I would suggest you take the time needed to gather the most accurate information possible to develop your business avatar. Here are a few ways:

- Use surveys to capture feedback from your existing customers.
- *Ask Your Target Market* (a leading innovator in DIY online market research) is a great solution for surveying a larger audience base.
- Adding a Custom Audience Pixel to your website is an effective way to track and learn more about people who have visited your website.
- Interviews capture valuable information and allow you to dive deeper into the answers given by asking "Why?" This lets you uncover the behaviors that drive the respondents.

Multiple Avatars

By now you might be thinking, "What if I have more than one avatar?" Having multiple avatars is perfectly fine. In fact, most businesses will have more than one ideal customer, especially if they offer more than one product or service.

The best way to define your customer avatars is to tackle them one at a time. I would suggest that you start with the market that brings the most profit to your business. (Good idea, right?)

Through this process, you may even find yourself realizing that your business is too broad and that you need to tighten up your product or service offering to develop your niche and position yourself to deliver your best to that market.

Negative Avatars

Creating a negative avatar can be as beneficial as creating your customer avatar. A negative avatar is a generalized representation of the persona that you don't want as a customer. Knowing who you don't want to serve as a customer can sometimes make it easier to know who you do want to serve.

If you want to start here, which is a good idea, I'd suggest you think of that one customer who was a total nightmare to work with, and document all of the things that made the relationship unsuccessful.

The key here is to not focus on personal characteristics that made the individual difficult to work with, but rather on the reasons why the customer wasn't a good fit for your product or service — high prices, the probability of increased churn, not being properly equipped for long-term success.

DEFINE YOUR CUSTOMER AVATAR

1. Demographic traits: list out your avatar's demographic traits (e.g., age, sex, education level, income level, marital status, occupation, religion, and average family size). This area is typically easy to define.
2. Psychographic traits: these are a little more complicated and require a deeper understanding of your client avatar. They're based on values, attitudes, interests, and lifestyles. Examples include wanting a healthy lifestyle, valuing time with family, using Pinterest to do home DIY projects.
3. Name your avatar: naming your avatar humanizes the profile.
4. Put a face to the name: find a picture online in stock photos that best represents what your avatar looks like.
5. Design a dossier: a dossier is a one-page collection of information about your avatar that includes its name, picture, information, and story.
6. Speaking of story: write one about your customer avatar. Imagine you are your avatar and are journaling about the discovery of your product or service. What were you thinking before you bought the product? How were you feeling? Why were you feeling that way? What were you looking for? What were you hoping to solve or accomplish? How did you find the product or hear about it? How did you feel once you purchased the product or service?

Takeaways

At the most basic level, developing a customer avatar will help you become more effective in your messaging and cut through the noise in today's marketing landscape. Using it in combination with a solid lifecycle marketing strategy is a surefire way to accelerate your business growth. Here are some steps to take as you begin developing your client avatar:

- Create a negative avatar first to gain clarity about who you don't want to serve as a customer and who isn't a good fit.
- Bring your customer avatar to life with a name, face, and personal story. Be as specific as possible — the more details you have, the better you and your perfect customer will connect.
- Tackle one customer avatar at a time.

- Create your avatar based on market research and customer feedback rather than your own opinion and perception.

Customer Avatar Surveys

By now, you should know the importance of having a customer avatar, but you may not be so sure about how to go about building one (or more).

One of the best ways to build a strong customer avatar is by creating and dispersing customer avatar surveys. Believe it or not, people still answer surveys. A well-built survey or questionnaire can help you gain some of the best feedback on your ideal customer.

One of the main reasons some surveys fail to gain useful information is their poor construction. Let's break down a few of the top customer avatar survey "don't do's" and help you start getting the feedback you need to create the perfect avatars.

Customer Avatar Survey No-No's

You can pour hours of time and effort into creating an excellent survey yet still have trouble getting people to complete and submit it.

A survey is only as valuable as the data you receive from it. If you are wondering why your survey isn't garnering the feedback you thought it would, you may be facing one or more of the following problems:

The Survey Is Too Long

Have you ever been strolling down Main Street and been approached by a well-meaning volunteer asking you to offer your opinion on a topic? They hand you a paper survey to fill out, and you gasp as you see 45 questions asking for your opinion and honest feedback.

My honest feedback on this type of survey? I don't want to do it. It's too long, and I've got places to be.

Even 20 questions are too many.

Keep your survey as short as possible — ideally five questions or fewer — while still designed to gain helpful insights and feedback on building your customer avatar. The faster and easier it is to complete, the more likely you are to get more results.

The Survey Isn't Clear

"When you came into the building, how did you feel?"

Wait — how do I feel about what exactly? *The customer service? The look and feel of the room? The amenities offered? The wait time? The napkin style?*

If your survey is filled with vague questions, it will likely elicit vague answers, and that won't give you much help in building a customer avatar. Keep your questions precise, pointed, and focused on the particular elements of your idea that you need feedback on.

The Survey Isn't Variable Enough

Ever sat down at a restaurant and had a waitress ask you to complete a customer satisfaction survey? Usually, you run into two types:

- The survey asks for your opinion on a few services with fill-in-the-dot numerical scales (1-10)
- The survey features open-ended questions with plenty of writing space below

In general, surveys with too much white space for users to input information manually are less effective at getting valuable data. The amount of work required to fill out a survey will directly impact the likelihood that the survey will be completed.

6 Top Online Survey Builders for Developing a Customer Avatar

Want to build a strong and effective survey for creating a customer avatar? There are many free online survey builders available, and finding the right one is essential.

If you aren't sure where to start, check out a list of the top online survey builders here: www.BrainToBank.com/Resources.

Experiment to Find the Best Survey Builder for You

What's the best survey builder for you? The answer to this question will depend largely on your needs. Are you looking for a free, online form-builder that can create surveys fast, or do you need more robust features and customization options in exchange for paying modest fees per month?

Take a look at each, give them all a try with a few test questions, and pick the best one for helping you bring your idea to your target audience.

"What Do I Get for Taking Your Survey?"

Do you really want to see results from your customer avatar survey? It's time to invest a few dollars in it.

One great way to get feedback is to incentivize your surveys. Offer something of value in return for full completion of the survey and you will increase your completion rates and get more valuable feedback. Gift cards, discounts on future products, you name it. Get creative with incentives.

CHAPTER 12 - Action Accelerators

THINK IT → ORGANIZE IT → DO IT

Take action on these items NOW to keep driving your idea from Brain to Bank:

1. Use surveys to capture feedback from your existing customers.
2. Use an online platform for surveying a larger audience base. See www.BrainToBank.com/Resources for suggestions.
3. Add a Custom Audience Pixel to your website as an effective way to track and learn more about people who have visited your website.
4. Interview your customers (or potential customers if you are just getting started). This lets you uncover the behaviors that drive them.
5. Now complete your ideal customer avatar in the Appendix section of this book or at www.BrainToBank.com/Resources.
6. Explore various online survey platforms to determine which one(s) best suit your needs. Conduct a test run.
7. Update your roadmap so it has the most current information.

STICK TO THE PLAN

Chapter 13

Distribution & Logistics

YOU'VE GOT A FINISHED PRODUCT...NOW WHAT?

Congratulations! You've finally finished that brilliant project you've been working on… the one you've poured your heart and soul into for years while experiencing sleepless nights and maybe even a panic attack or two. Well, all that's about to pay off.

Now that you've got a finished product in your hands (or in the cloud), it's time to go back to the drawing board, but this time with a brand-new sketchbook. It's time to figure out how you're going to get this product into the hands of the masses.

OEM Supply Agreements

An Original Equipment Manufacturer (also known as an OEM) is a company that produces parts and equipment to be marketed by another manufacturer. One example is Foxconn, a Taiwanese electronics company that manufactures parts and equipment for other companies such as Apple, Dell, Google, Nokia, and Nintendo.

An OEM agreement is a contractual relationship between one or more companies in which the OEM provides another manufacturer with a product they will then market themselves.

For example, a computer manufacturer, Company A, has a requirement for a high-performance graphics card for its computer systems. Instead of developing the graphics card in-house, Company A enters into an OEM agreement with a graphics card manufacturer, Company B.

Under the OEM agreement, Company B will manufacture the graphics card according to Company A's specifications and supply it to Company A on a regular basis. Company A will then integrate the graphics card into its computer systems and market and sell the computers under its own brand name. Company B will not be involved in the marketing or sales of the computers, and its graphics card will not be marketed or sold under its own brand name.

In this example, Company B is the OEM, and Company A is the company that is rebranding and selling the product. The OEM agreement allows Company A to obtain a high-performance graphics card without having to develop it in-house, while allowing Company B to increase its production capacity and generate additional revenue. This arrangement is beneficial for both companies, as it allows them to focus on their core business activities and benefit from economies of scale.

Before signing an OEM Supply Agreement, consider the following:

- **Branding**
  Will the OEM market your brand or will they expect to use their own? Depending on the type of product you have and the financial compensation offered, you might not mind taking your name off of the product — a condition commonly referred to as a licensing agreement. However, if you're looking to grow your own business and want your branding intact, this is something to be negotiated.

- **Payment**
  Will you be compensated for your product up front, or will you get a percentage of each sale the secondary manufacturer makes? Make sure you know how much and when you'll get paid. It's a good idea to consult your CPA on this aspect of the contract.

- **Duration of Contract**
  It may be an advantage if you've never worked with this particular manufacturer before to sign a short contract. You'll have a chance to see how it goes and if the manufacturing partnership is working as expected. On the other hand, signing a longer contract can be attractive because you will have a longer commitment and you'll know the pricing for a specific period of time. You'll need to weigh your options and take your best guess on what the duration of the contract should be. Since you are a new company, the OEM may be telling you, and you'll have little say in the matter.

- **Intellectual Property Protection**
  Will your product be protected under the terms of your contract? How much access will the secondary manufacturer have to your intellectual property? As always, consulting your IP attorney is advisable.

Signing an OEM Supply Agreement can be a great way to grow your business. However, do err on the side of caution and go into the negotiation process with a great contract lawyer so you can be protected and strike the best deal possible.

Another Episode in the Entrepreneur Drama Series
I Didn't See It Coming

I worked with a company out of Southern California that picked up a North American distribution for aftermarket auto parts. The corporation contracting the new North American distribution company was headquartered in Dubai, and the manufacturing came out of Australia.

There were five equal partners in the newly developed organization, all with diverse backgrounds and specific responsibilities: one with operations expertise, one with warehouse and logistics experience, others with sales.

One of the founders had expertise with OEMs and distribution, so he headed up that part of the company.

One of the biggest problems with their business model was how to stock their new business. They had no idea how many units of which automobile models they would need, or when. "Just in time" ordering was not an option, as each model variable of the product took too long to measure, make, and distribute.

Time to delivery took far too long and was killing the business; for their customers, it was like ordering a Starbucks coffee and then having to go back in a few weeks to pick it up. Who wants that?

Additionally, after factoring in distribution costs, they couldn't get enough return on their investment without raising prices, which made the goods not competitive with similar products currently on the market.

To make matters worse, behind the backs of the other four founders the partner in charge of distribution was going around the salespeople and making his own deals with OEMs, thus cutting out commissions rightfully owed to his partners.

So, even if you're not the person in charge of distribution, you want to fully understand this aspect of your operation. Do the numbers; is that final number red or black? Don't get stuck stocking a lot of inventory. Keep the number of products you have to distribute down; one is a good number to start with. And oh, be careful who you chose for your distribution partner. Just sayin'.

Define Potential Distributors – Domestic and International

Before you find a distributor, whether domestic, international, or both, you must do plenty of research:

- Discover what it is you want out of a distributor
- Determine who will be able to fulfill all of your business needs and wants

Here's how you can do this:

1. Create an "ideal distributor" avatar
   This is just like creating the ideal customer avatar you completed in Chapter 12. Develop a checklist that includes all of the criteria a distributor needs to meet for you to reach your goals. Having a well-thought-out checklist will help you narrow your search, keep you focused, and save you lots of time.

2. Reach out
   Start by sending an email to each potential distributor you are considering, giving a brief introduction to yourself, your company, and your product. Tell the potential distributor that you will be in town on (give date) to conduct market research, and you would love to set up an in-person interview. If the

location is too far for you to conveniently travel, ask to set up a phone or video interview.

3. Re-Strategize
   If you don't get the answer you were hoping for from a potential distributor, don't be discouraged. Even if someone is not interested in your initial offer, that person may recommend another potential distributor you hadn't previously thought of. The answer "no" is not the sound of a door slamming — it's an opportunity to travel down another road. Think Robert Frost.

4. Gather references
   Before you choose a distributor who looks perfect on paper, ask around for some references from other suppliers. This background check should include overall experiences as well as payment history and will help save your company many headaches later.

Consider Industry Strategic Partners for Distribution

Create a list of potential partnerships with distributors in your industry. The list you make will be similar to what you created in Chapter 3.

As you may recall, a strategic partnership is an agreed-upon collaboration between businesses that have similar goals. The ability to distinguish between conventional alliances and those that are truly strategic is a talent to be mastered.

This partnership is symbiotic in that it benefits both parties to combine efforts, resources, and information to help each other get an edge in the marketplace. Find distributors with needs and goals that might sync with yours and approach them to see if they are a good strategic fit for distribution.

Some of the many benefits of creating strategic distribution partnerships include:

- Increased Revenue
- Expanded Customer Base
- Expanded Geographic Reach
- Extended Product Lines (cross-selling)
- Shared Resources
- Access to New Technologies and IP

Signing an OEM Supply Agreement can be a great way to grow your business. However, do err on the side of caution and go into the negotiation process with a great contract lawyer so you can be protected and strike the best deal possible.

Should I Consider 3PL?

A growing trend in eCommerce and entrepreneurship is partnering with a third-party logistics (3PL) company. Whether you are offering an innovative product or opening an eCommerce store, finding a partner who can help you navigate the world of global logistics is key to success.

Once you have found and are satisfied with an OEM, you will start to see products flying off the manufacturing floor and into the hands of distribution and logistics. While you may decide to hold and store products in your home or office, there could be a better option with a logistics expert who knows how to help small businesses and entrepreneurs thrive: a third-party logistics company.

What Does A 3PL Offer?

You may not be quite ready for the level of logistics processing a 3PL offers but understanding how this type of company operates can help you save tons of time and money in the future.

In short, 3PL companies are all about one thing: outsourcing.

Remember when we discussed outsourcing your development tasks in Chapter 7? Outsourcing is still an important part of your business growth process — even once your products are in production.

Partnering with a high-quality 3PL company can help you manage your business logistics seamlessly. This allows you to spend more time focusing on the parts of running and growing your business that you are passionate about.

When you team up with a 3PL service, you will find a business partner who can help cover a variety of logistics aspects:

Product Sourcing

It's important for eCommerce businesses to be able to automatically source products from an OEM for order fulfillment. Sourcing products is a time-consuming process, but a 3PL can take care of it as needed — and potentially offer insights about other manufacturers who can help to scale your business.

Warehousing

Products are created; products are sent out to customers. What happens in between? A 3PL will offer warehousing services, storing your products on their site so you don't have to find a place to keep boxes upon boxes of your great idea in your basement.

Order Fulfillment

If you are selling your products online, certain 3PLs can automatically track orders, pick products, and ship your brilliant idea out to the world. Another great way to save time and money on storage and shipping costs.

Analytics & Reporting

How many products are you selling this month? How many of those are going out to customers via mail, UPS, FedEx, etc.? The last thing you want to do is simply push GO and start an endless stream of product manufacturing. Rather than opening the faucet and letting it run, a 3PL team will offer reporting and analytics services that will keep you up to date on your latest numbers, and help you pivot as necessary.

Growth & Scaling Features

As you (hopefully) grow and scale your business, you will eventually need to consider the cost and effort involved in scaling your operation. Your 3PL will work with you to offer more warehousing, sourcing, and fulfillment options as you grow — so you don't have to figure it out along the way.

You may not be ready to hire a full-service 3PL yet, but you will at some point need some logistical superpowers should your idea go from brain to bank and beyond.

CHAPTER 13 - Action Accelerators

THINK IT ⟶ ORGANIZE IT ⟶ DO IT

Take action on these items NOW to keep driving your idea from Brain to Bank:

1. Decide what you want out of a distribution partnership as well as what you're going to bring to the table.

2. Create your "ideal distributor avatar" and begin researching companies that may fit into your vision. Make a list.

3. Create your ideal distributor avatar using the worksheet here: www.BrainToBank.com/Resources.

4. Decide how much inventory you need to keep on hand. Can you do "just in time?"

5. Do the numbers. Is that final number acceptable after factoring in needed inventory, distribution, and logistics costs?

6. Can you keep the number of product items you have to distribute down to only one to begin with? For example, if you're selling candles, can you start with the Vanilla Cinnamon Latte scent first and see how it goes?

7. Be sure to do your due diligence on the distribution partners you are considering. How long have they been in business? What other companies do they distribute for? What is their financial stability? Their reputation? Talk to other customers who use their services. What did you learn?

8. Investigate 3PLs and determine the best ones that you may use now or in the future.

9. Update your roadmap so it has the most current information.

STICK TO THE PLAN

Chapter 14

Marketing to the Masses

EXTRA! EXTRA! READ ALL ABOUT IT!

When you're preparing to create your marketing plan, the most important word these days is "digital." We could spend time discussing television ads, radio, and print, but the biggest bang for your buck is digital. But you already know this.

This wasn't the case when I started my first business at age 8. Instead of selling common and boring lemonade, my brother Steve and I decided to invent a new product: Cubesicles®. Just kidding about the ®!

Cubesicles were made by pouring various flavors of Kool-Aid® (real registration) into a metal ice cube tray. Halfway through the freezing process we inserted a toothpick in each one. Voila! New product.

Now, how do we get the word out?

To begin with, we let all of our friends know, and asked them to let their friends know. We put up posters. We rode our bikes down the street launching flyers paper-airplane style, shouting, Extra! Extra! Read all about it!

In this day and age, we still use these marketing strategies, usually sans bikes and shouting. The new "word of mouth" method is best accomplished on the World Wide Web, which has the biggest "mouth" and the widest reach.

In the past, I have resisted utilizing social media sites. But I have had to learn to embrace this ultra-fast and effective way of marketing because I insist on succeeding. If you are someone who has been slow to adopt social media, just remember that it is a necessary, timely, and smart strategic part of your victory plan. Digital media have surpassed web pages in influence, just as web pages superseded the texting that replaced email years ago.

I have found tremendous benefits in embracing digital media. They outweigh the negatives, including the negative sense of spending an inordinate amount of time and money on my digital devices. I realize those devices and their apps get my info out there much more quickly, and to a larger audience, than I ever could using conventional methods.

I'd encourage you to go on Instagram, Facebook, YouTube, and Twitter and explore how some of the most successful people and companies let social media do the talking for them. Explore, analyze, and then implement what excites and works for you.

If digital marketing and social media sites are not something you are adept at using or want to spend time learning and/or doing, remember the lesson on "Who Not How" in Chapter 7. However, if you do decide to implement this powerful digital behemoth, you'll find the Internet is your best friend when it comes to marketing your product.

Understanding the Language of Digital Marketing

When you look into creating a digital marketing campaign for your business, it's essential to know marketing buzzwords that will help your campaign succeed. These essential marketing terms are valuable in helping you create and better understand your promotion.

ADVICE FROM INDUSTRY EXPERTS

WebFX, a highly successful digital marketing firm, offers these basic marketing terms to help you understand the ever-evolving digital marketing world:[24]

1. **Brand Identity**

   Definition:
   Your business's persona, style, and reputation online.

   Where you'll commonly hear this term:
   When designing your website or running a social media campaign.

   As you look at different marketing jargon, you'll come across the term *brand identity*.

   Your brand identity is how you establish your business to your customers.

You want your business to be unique and stand out from its competitors. Having a brand identity allows you to determine what's unique about your business.

You can build your brand identity through:

- Page copy
- Logo
- Web design choices
- Imagery

Brand identity is vital to your business because it influences your audience's impression of your business. If you build a strong brand identity, your audience will get a sense of who you are and your business's values.

2. **Click Through Rate (CTR)**

Definition:

How many clicks your ad receives per number of impressions.

Where you'll commonly hear this term:

When running ads, optimizing for search engines, and running email campaigns.

Clickthrough rate (CTR) is an important metric when you're running advertising campaigns. CTR is the ratio of people who click on your media compared with those who merely view it.

> **CTR** is the ratio of people who **click on your media** Compared to **those who only view it**.

This metric is crucial for your business because it helps you see the effectiveness of your campaign. Your CTR can show you whether you effectively drive people to click on your content.

3. **Conversion Rate Optimization (CRO)**
Definition:
Improving the percentage of web users who turn into paying customers.

Where you'll commonly hear this term:
Whenever you use a strategy that helps you earn conversions, like PPC or email marketing.

If your projected conversion rate is low, conversion rate optimization can help you refine the conversion process to drive more sales for your business.

Let's say you're running a PPC campaign and find your ad is earning conversions as you expected. Upon analyzing your ad, you may find there are certain features on your ad that deter leads. By using CRO, you optimize your ad to alter these elements and improve your conversion rate.

4. **Customer Relationship Management (CRM)**
Definition:
Software that helps you track customer information and interactions with your business.

Where you'll commonly hear this term:
When you're starting to create campaigns for digital marketing strategies and want an easy way to manage information about your audience.

Customer relationship management (CRM) is a common term you'll hear when you run a digital marketing campaign. This software helps you get to know your customers better so you can create digital campaigns that resonate with them.

5. **Geofencing Marketing**
Definition:
Location-based marketing that uses invisible barriers that allow you to target people directly.

Where you'll commonly hear this term:
When creating any local marketing strategy, such as a local SEO.

"Geofencing" is an essential piece of marketing jargon. You'll often hear this term when people discuss creating a local SEO campaign.

When you use geofencing, you create an invisible fence around your business or a competitor's business. After you create the barrier, you can send users text messages, deliver in-app notifications, or show social media ads. You do this when a user enters or exits the virtual fence.

This strategy allows you to deliver relevant information directly to your audience. You can share information that gets your audience to visit your business. The only catch with this strategy is that people must turn on their location on their mobile devices.

Geofencing has grown increasingly popular with apps like Facebook. It's important to know about it as it becomes a more integral part of local marketing.

6. **Earned Media**

When you're running a digital marketing campaign, you'll encounter three types of media: owned, paid, and earned. While owned and paid media are relatively self-explanatory, many people aren't clear on what earned media is.

Definition:

Things that others write or circulate about your business, media you have not paid for or created yourself. Earned media is other people telling your audience about your business.

Where you'll commonly hear this term:

In blogging or social media marketing. Many people call earned media "word-of-mouth marketing."

Earned media is any marketing done for your business that you aren't involved in creating. Many people call earned media "word-of-mouth marketing." Earned media is other people telling your audience about your business.

Some examples of earned media include:

- Social mentions
- Social shares
- Reviews
- Reposted content

With all of these, your audience voluntarily shares your business or your information with their friends and family. It's an excellent way for you to gain brand exposure and reach more people interested in your business.

This term is one of the most critical marketing terms to know because of how it impacts your audience. People consider earned media a trusted source of information about your business, because it's coming from someone other than you. As you build your marketing strategy, get familiar with earned media.

7. **Key Performance Indicators (KPIs)**

Definition:
Important metrics that determine the success of your campaign.

Where you'll commonly hear this term:
When you use any digital marketing strategy; all of them require choosing KPIs to indicate success.

If you've ever met with a digital marketing company, you've probably heard them use this term; it's one of the most popular marketing buzzwords. Key performance indicators (KPIs) allow your business to see where your campaign succeeds and where it falls short.

These KPIs help you understand whether people like your campaigns and how they interact with your content. You can analyze KPIs to see if you need to make improvements to your campaign, and where you should make them.

If you're going to run a digital marketing campaign, you must know basic marketing terms. KPIs is a primary marketing term that will help you better understand your campaign and how it drives results for your business.

Some common KPIs include:

- Organic growth
- Clicks
- Conversions
- Downloads

8. **Marketing Automation**

Definition:
Software that enables you to systematize certain marketing processes to save yourself time and money.

Where you'll commonly hear this term:
Anytime you run a digital marketing campaign.

Marketing automation is another essential marketing buzzword. When you invest in digital marketing, you'll quickly learn how involved and intricate it is. You won't have enough manpower and resources to manage every aspect of your campaigns.

This is where marketing automation comes into play. Marketing automation allows you to perform crucial key marketing functions without having to dedicate the manpower and extra resources.

This software helps you complete processes such as:

- Customer segmentation
- Email automation
- Campaign management
- Analytics
- Reporting

Instead of spending a lot of personal time and resources, you'll save them by using marketing automation software. It's important to know the name of this powerful marketing tool because it strongly impacts how you run your campaigns.

9. **Mobile Optimization**

Definition:
The process of optimizing media to look good and function well on mobile devices.

Where you'll commonly hear this term:
When building your website's design.

Mobile optimization should be an integral part of your digital marketing vocabulary — and plan. People use their mobile devices more than ever to conduct searches, find businesses, and buy products. If you want to appeal to these customers, mobile optimization is the key.

This digital marketing tool helps your business create more mobile-friendly pages.

One example of mobile optimization is a responsive design. A responsive design enables your site to adapt to whatever device a customer uses. This process means that your website will adjust to fit the mobile user's screen, creating a better experience for your audience. Mobile optimization includes the mobile-friendly features and elements you integrate into your design.

10. Personalization

Definition:

Providing your audience with a unique experience by creating marketing materials that appeal to specific groups.

Where you'll commonly hear this term:

When you're creating an email marketing campaign.

Personalization is one of the most critical marketing buzzwords you'll hear in digital marketing. It describes how you use customization to create a unique experience for different members of your audience.

With personalization, you take the approach of creating a unique experience for different members of your audience.

People come to your business for different reasons. If you owned a photography company, you'd have people interested in engagement photo shoots, wedding shoots, maternity shoots, and more. Because people want your products or services for a variety of reasons, it's essential to tailor each experience to what the customer wants.

Your company can personalize each audience experience by sending customers only pertinent information relevant to their interests.

If someone were interested in your wedding photoshoots, you could send them information about your affordable wedding packages. You could also send your portfolio of previous wedding shoots or information about how to hire the right photographer for their wedding.

11. **Retargeting**

Definition:

Showing users ads for products or services they viewed previously to get them to convert.

Where you'll commonly hear this term:

When running paid advertising campaigns, such as PPC ads and social media ads.

Retargeting is one of the primary marketing concepts that has a substantial impact on your business's conversion rate. This strategy helps you obtain conversions you may have otherwise lost.

Retargeted ads show products or services to users they viewed previously. Many people will see products and need more time to consider. In the process, many users forget what product they were looking at, which can result in a loss of conversions.

With retargeting, the ads encourage people to think about that product or service again. If they're close to conversion, it could be the final prod that gets them to convert.

12. **Return On Investment (ROI)**

Definition:

The money your business gets back from investing in digital marketing strategies as it pertains to marketing (not your business as a whole).

Where you'll commonly hear this term:

Any time you run a digital marketing campaign.

Return on Investment (ROI) is a common marketing buzzword that refers to how much money your business receives through investing in different digital marketing strategies.

Your ROI is a crucial indicator of your business's success. If you have a high ROI, it means that you're getting more money back than you're investing to help your business grow. A low ROI indicates you're spending too much to market your business, and your profit suffers as a result.

13. **User Experience**

Definition:

How your audience positively or negatively interacts with your business online.

Where you'll commonly hear this term:

You'll frequently hear this term when designing your website, but it applies to all aspects of your digital marketing campaign.

User experience is a critical component of success for your digital marketing campaign. It's one of the marketing concepts focused on improving your audience's experience on your site.

If users don't have a positive experience on your website, you could lose them to the competition. To keep users engaged with your site and excited about your content, you have to provide them with a stellar user experience.

You influence user experience through graphics and videos on your pages, your site's ease of navigation, even the number of internal links you feature.

These site elements work together to create an experience that users will enjoy and remember.

This marketing jargon is essential to know because it helps you create more refined campaigns that please your audience, which ultimately results in more sales and profits.

How to Do Marketing

This was the first subheading of this chapter. Now, let's go back to one of the first lessons you learned and change it: it's not HOW… it's WHO.

Who to Hire to Do Marketing

I recently worked with a nonprofit organization that had very little money to spend on marketing and couldn't get traction without it. They suggested that high school students be hired to do the marketing. After all, teens are cheap, and they really understand electronics. Their CFO — keeper and protector of the funds — retorted, "I'd rather spend more money and get someone really good."

There you have it from one whose job is to spend as little as possible. Spend the money and get someone who knows what they are doing. As in all things, you'll get what you pay for.

Unless you're an expert marketer, spend the money rather than do it yourself. To quote Dan Sullivan of Strategic Coaching, it's always "Who Not How."

Whoa, Whoa - What's SEO?

While I will take the liberty of assuming you are familiar with digital marketing and online branding — since you are reading this book — I don't want to fly past the digital marketing service station without stopping for gas.

Search engine optimization (SEO) is a buzzword that is often thrown around as if it were digital marketing's "golden ticket." Like a drive down the Vegas Strip, your foray into digital marketing will see you encounter a variety of such flashy ideas promising instant success.

But what is SEO — and should you invest time and effort in making sure your SEO is phenomenal? Let's break down the concept of search engine optimization and why it may be one of the most important investments you can make at this point in your journey.

SEO, SERP, and Local Pack

When consumers hop online to search for a product or service, one of the first places they will likely head is their browser. They will type what they are looking for into the small search bar, and — like magic — Google will offer an endless stream of options for that particular search term.

As you bring your idea from brain to bank you will want to make sure your product is being seen first when someone searches your category. With users making fast purchase decisions online, if you aren't at the top of the search engine results page (SERP), you are likely leaving money on the table.

Across your website and social media presence, SEO will help you increase your visibility by assisting Google to find your content. Whether through particular keywords or phrases on your website pages or with backend metadata, you can give Google a helping hand in searching across your content by optimizing your digital marketing.

SEO is such a powerful digital marketing tool that Google has introduced a SERP capability known as the Local Pack. The Local Pack contains settings and information you can put in your My Google business account to help your company name and information quickly show up at the top of any search. Google is tightening the availability of the Local Pack — from a large group of seven top spots to three, with the company testing out only two spots right now.

Feel the pressure to be seen? The more you optimize, the more you open the doors to potential customers and success across the globe.

Outsource Your SEO

Sounds like a lot of work? Maybe, if you aren't already familiar with how SEO operates. So, what do we do when we want to see success in an area of business we aren't particularly familiar with?

Ding-Ding! You've got it! OUTSOURCE! (Okay, I know I gave it away in the subtitle.)

There are many SEO and digital marketing gurus out on the market who are ready to step in and help you boost your online performance. Revisit Chapter 7 to remind yourself of the steps to take when hiring out your work and partnering with a contractor, in this case a digital agency that can quickly supercharge your SEO in just a few hours. As you grow your business, an SEO expert can help you keep up and compete in the market by making sure you always show up at the top of the search results.

CHAPTER 14 - Action Accelerators

THINK IT ⟶ ORGANIZE IT ⟶ DO IT

Take action on these items NOW to keep driving your idea from Brain to Bank:

1. Do research (or have a "Who" do this) and find the right person or company to do your marketing.
2. Determine which marketing automation software you will use. Get a trial and check it out to make sure it will meet your needs.
3. Create an initial game plan for a pre-launch marketing. Do an A/B test to make sure you are on the right track.[25]
4. Create a one-year and also a three-year plan for continued marketing.
5. Update your roadmap so it has the most current information.

STICK TO THE PLAN

Chapter 15
The Race to Profitability

TURNING A PROFIT IN THE FIRST 100 DAYS

"Looks easy, does hard." A former partner of mine used to quote this whenever the topic of money came up. It's true, turning a profit as a new business is hard... but it's not impossible. There are strategies for turning a profit in under six months. Forget the typical estimation of two or three years, who has time for that? The world is changing faster than ever, and you need to establish yourself as a profitable business as soon as possible.

Hence, our goal of 100 days or less.

Photo credits Giorgio Trovato (money) and Mockaroon (calendar)

When you set the goal to turn a profit in 100 days or less, you become relentless in the pursuit of that goal. If something or someone stands in your way, you've got your end goal in mind and you go around, over, under, or through to achieve it.

Without this economic push, projects usually go on and on and on, never reaching profitability.

Another Episode in the Entrepreneurial Drama Series *I Didn't See It Coming*

I worked with a SaaS technology company that had been creating a software platform for the financial industry — commonly referred to as FinTech — for several years. The Chief Operations Officer (COO) was overseeing the project and was very much engaged with the process. Although not an IT project or product manager by trade or education, he'd read a lot of articles on the internet and felt up to the challenge.

He believed "agile" was the new and improved way of working. The old waterfall approach of having deadlines and meeting them was old school.

The biggest problem was that he had never worked on an agile development team before, and he didn't understand how to properly utilize this method. His many Internet readings on the agile method for IT development were interpreted by him to mean that improvements and iterations were to be implemented whenever they arose.

Agile project management is indeed an iterative approach to delivering a project throughout its life cycle. Iterative or agile life cycles are composed of several iterations or incremental steps toward the completion of a project.

Iterative approaches are frequently used in software development projects to accelerate adaptability, since the benefit of iteration is that you can adjust as you go along rather than following a linear path.

However, using the agile method does not mean you can change anything and everything whenever you like. Agile is all about change, but change within reason. When scope is not kept in mind, both time and money suffer.

The COO had not kept the original scope in mind. After 10 years the company did not have a viable SaaS product, nor was it making a profit.

3,650 days later... way past 100 days... the company still was not profitable. All of that is what *not* to do.

Do this instead:

- ✓ Do the research. Determine what you will build = scope. Stick to the scope.
- ✓ Research how long similar products have taken to build. Set your timeline. Stick to the timeline.
- ✓ Research how much your product should cost. Stick to the numbers.
- ✓ Stick to the plan.

What to Charge

Pricing your product or service is one of the core decisions you'll make when preparing your financial pro formas. The price you set is a pivotal element in all of your financials, from cash flow to profit margin to which expenses you decide to cover.

Pricing isn't a decision you only make once. The best pricing data you can get comes from launching your product and testing with real customers. Then you can adjust your price from what you learn.

The most important element of your price is that it needs to sustain your business. If you price your products at a loss, or an unsustainable profit margin, you're going to find it challenging to grow and scale. You'll also most likely find yourself out of business.

There are other important factors that your pricing needs to take into consideration. For example, how does your price compare to your competitors' prices? Will your ideal customer be able to get a similar product or service from a competitor? If there are major differences in the products, what are they? If your product is better, your price should be slightly higher.

What about customers' expectations? Your customers will not be solely motivated by price; they will also be weighing value. Your marketing should establish why your product is better, not by listing features but by explaining what it will do for the customer. How your product benefits the customer is your value proposition, not the bells and whistles.

To set your price, first calculate your sustainable base price:

1. Add up your variable costs
2. Add a profit margin
3. Add in fixed costs

Make sure you know your cost-per-unit; include shipping and other costs involved in getting your product out the door.

Don't let anxiety over posting the "wrong" price hold you back from launching your product. As long as your number covers expenses and delivers an acceptable profit, you can test and adjust as you go.

Here's the thing: pricing is always going to evolve with your business. Once you have a price that helps you build a viable business, you can launch your new product. Use the feedback and data you get from customers to adjust your pricing strategy in the future.

Rinse. Repeat.

AVOID MAKING FINANCIAL MISTAKES

Being smart about setting your price, and then resetting it as things evolve is something you do. To turn a profit in 100 days or less, it's just as important to *not* do certain things. Some of these don't-do items include:

Spending Money on Expensive Office Space

When your mind, spouse, or business partner says, "But we have to have a nice place to meet clients," remind them of the many "garage start-ups" that didn't.

Splurging on "Impressive" Furniture

When you're told... once again... "But we have to look like we're successful... you know, 'fake it 'til you make it,'" remind them that these days, except for the offices of doctors, lawyers, and other well-papered professionals, few workplaces are overrun with visitors.

Giving Your Profit Away

Don't give away "free samples" or discount your product. You may be tempted to do that to stimulate interest and growth, but you'll quickly find you can't profit without charging users something up front.

Hiring W2 Employees Too Soon

Remember our chapter on outsourcing and virtual assistants? Did you know you can even outsource Human Resources and CFOs? You'd be amazed how long you can stay in this "temp" mode... sometimes forever. You can hire the right people for the tasks and positions you need by testing them out first, and then when the time is right, you can add them as employees.

Note: The IRS has strict rules about who qualifies as a contracted 1099 worker and who is an actual company employee. Make sure you know the rules and abide by them.

Contractor or Employee? How to Determine the Difference

As you continue to build and scale your business, there will inevitably come a time when you need to bring on other help. In the early days, you most likely worked closely with freelancers or contractors to complete tasks and take your idea to the next level. These contractors were invaluable individuals who brought a select set of skills and abilities to your business when permanent employees were financially out of your reach.

However, you may discover it is more beneficial to bring on an individual as a long-term employee. You can train and build up an employee into someone who knows your company, your goals, and your leadership — rather than having to reinvent that wheel with every new contractor.

Not sure how to define a particular individual as a 1099 contractor or an actual employee? Start with the entity that will likely care the most: the Internal Revenue Service. The IRS will be interested in how you are designating particular individuals in your company, especially as you pay them.

Let's take a look at the main ways the IRS determines employed status:

Behavioral Control

In general, the IRS designates a worker as a company's employee when the company owner has the ability to control and direct the work performed by that individual. Some of the more prominent determiners are:

- **Giving of Specific Working Instructions:** this can include where to buy tools, how to purchase supplies, and where or when the individual should work.
- **The Detail of Instruction Given:** employees will receive more precise working instructions, which showcases control.
- **Set Evaluations of the Individual:** the company uses evaluation systems to track and monitor performance.
- **Training of Workers:** employees will often receive formal training on how to complete their work.

Financial Control

Another important aspect to consider is financial control. A worker is considered an employee if the business holds the right to direct and/or control the financial elements of a worker's role:

- The company invests in the equipment the employee uses.
- An employee cannot offer the same services to the free market during their employment.
- An employee is typically paid a consistent wage for hours worked, whereas a contractor will operate on a per-job basis or for a flat fee.

Relationship

Most importantly, a worker can be defined as an employee or as a contractor based on the type of relationship they maintain with the company:

- Contracts will often lay out the specific type of work the employee or contractor is offering.
- If an individual is an employee, the company will often offer employee benefits, including medical, vacation, and pension pay.
- Employees typically operate under a long-term paid status, while a contractor will offer services for a set period of time.

While these criteria are by no means exhaustive, it is important you understand and designate workers as either employees or contractors. Failing to do so can result in financial issues down the road, especially when it comes to tax time.

If you want to learn more about whether an individual working for you should be a contractor or an employee, check out the IRS website and research: Independent Contractor (Self-Employed) or Employee?

Your corporate attorney can also be a great resource for helping you identify employees vs. contractors.

NAOMI WATTS HAS NOTHING ON ME

In 2007, one of my sisters and I visited seven countries in 30 days on the African continent. Silverback gorilla trekking in Rwanda remains one of the highlights of that trip.

During a two-day exploration and silverback-seeking adventure, our small, global group observed entire clans of indigenous mountain gorillas that included several females with babies, adolescents and juveniles, and a massive silverback male, or as the guides called him, The Boss, who watched diligently over his growing troop.

The first group we encountered, Group 13, were quite docile, even The Boss, who was over 40 years old and lounged leisurely on his very silver back in a meadow, chewing on a bamboo stick. He couldn't have cared less that we were lurking close by observing his every move. I snapped dozens of photos of him alone in the open field, and then later of him with various females, mothers and their babies, and juveniles swinging in the trees. I felt like a National Geographic photographer on assignment.

The group we visited the next day was quite a different story. It was called "Group Hirwa," which means "lucky." This was the newest band in the jungle, with the youngest silverback. This boss had formed his small troop of eight females and subsequent juveniles and babies by stealing each female from another band. He was spectacular! Young and 400 pounds of muscle, intellect, and intuition, he was particularly watchful that another silverback wouldn't do the same to him.

Needless to say, the silverback in this group was not as happy to see us. He evaded my every attempt to grab a photo. He stayed hidden in the trees but watched us intently. Try as I might, I could not get a picture of him.

He ogled us from the perimeters for a time and then decided he had had enough and was going to go full-on alpha. He suddenly rushed onto the path where we were hiking and stood just below us glaring. Seeing his unexpected movement, our guide immediately yelled at us to get off the trail and stand quietly to the side and then not make any noise and not move.

Standing in the front row, I had my Nikon camera dangling from a strap around my neck and was itching to grab this photo op. I stood frozen, gripping the edges of my camera as I ever-so-slightly glanced up to see where he was, and could I please oh please snap this photo? When I looked up, I was staring right at him not 40 yards away.

The Boss looked me in the eye and I looked him in the eye, and then without warning, he bolted toward me. In a flash, he knuckle-bounded toward our group, straight at me, and quickly punched me with his gigantic, hairy fist, knocking me into the frightened trekkers behind me. I would have been knocked to the ground if someone had not been standing directly behind me.

The armed guides were so stunned they had no time to react. In hindsight, I now realize if they were going to shoot their rifles, it would have been at me, not the gorilla. He was, after all, $500 per trekker x 52 x 365 days. The gorilla had the upper hand… so to speak.

The guides commanded us to immediately vacate the jungle. As we were leaving the area, the young and mighty silverback followed us down the trail until we reached the clearing. He guarded the trail leading into the jungle so we could not go back up. Then he suddenly stormed out of the bamboo and marched toward us again. I could feel my heart beating in my throat, as I thought he was coming after me again.

The guide yelled to us to crouch down so we were lower in stature than The Boss. I got down all right... in back of the guide so I wouldn't be out front again, and ducked my blond head. The image of Naomi Watts being hauled off by King Kong flashed in my mind and it didn't look that fun. Finally, The Boss halted and waited and watched us leave until he could no longer see us.

All in all, it was a fabulous experience. Only 52 tourists a day are allowed to visit this endangered species, and I got to be one of them. Yes, I am very *hirwa*, as in very lucky. And yes, I am keeping that gigantic handprint on my clothes as proof that I was not touched by an angel, but attacked by a silverback gorilla!
Oh, and I got the photo. King Kong has nothing on him.

As you have so masterfully surmised, the name of any game involving a big, hairy beast — whether that be an actual silverback gorilla or the business beast of long hours, moments of mental exhaustion, and endless criticism and doubt from others — is Remember Your *Why* and Stay Focused.

Even when your end goal is temporarily out of sight, it's still there hiding in the underbrush of a little more effort, a few more iterations, or collaborating with an expert to ensure accuracy and deployment.

You get what you set out to get when you set out to get it. Now go get it.

CHAPTER 15 - Action Accelerators

THINK IT ⟶ ORGANIZE IT ⟶ DO IT

1. Decide how you will turn a profit in 100 days or less. Calculate your sustainable base price. Know your cost-per-unit. Are you still making a profit?

2. Think about where you want to be long-term and think of incremental growth and a steady plan to increase profit. What can you do today, this week, or this month to start improving your quality of profit ratio? Add these dates and milestones to your roadmap.

3. If you're not currently profitable, identify what's preventing you from making the money you know you're capable of earning. Once you've identified what is holding you back from your plan to increase profit, you can seek out the personal or professional tools needed to break through your barriers.

4. If a lack of growth is a problem within your sales team, think about how you can improve it. Do you need to hire fresh talent? Do you need to offer more incentives or make changes to the company culture to turn your team into raving fans of the business? Who supports you 100 percent? Who not only knows the company inside and out but can also rally the troops and bring in new customers? When you assemble a team of people who are excited to work for your brand and spread the message, it becomes much easier to be successful.

   If the problem is not within your team, it could be your product or the way you're marketing it that's not connecting with your target market. Once you've identified the areas in your business where you can optimize growth, you can be strategic about making impactful changes.

5. Strategically innovate. To do this, you need to identify who your customer is and why they need your product or service.

6. Identify how to truly add value your ideal customer can't ignore. Revisit your Customer Avatar worksheet and prioritize your market research to understand your customer's lifestyle and taste. By understanding your customer's mind and preferences, you're able to create compelling innovations customized to your market.

7. Understanding how to make a profit means taking a close look at how you're engaging your target market. There is no one-size-fits-all sales or marketing strategy, and you must customize yours to fit your product and clientele. Engage your target market digitally through your website and social media so they can easily access and learn about your product.

8. Create a timeline and develop a series of steps you and your team will take to increase your profit margin. Set reasonable goals you can sustain over time. Make a massive action plan that will help you jumpstart growth and increase profit at your business. Challenge yourself to turn a profit in 100 days or less.

9. Avoid making financial mistakes. Are any of the mentioned "money wasters" on your list of things to do? If so, make adjustments.

10. Update your roadmap so it has the most current information.

STICK TO THE PLAN

Chapter 16

Crossing the Finish Line

KEEP YOUR BUTT IN THE SADDLE

I've never ridden in the famous Iron Butt Rally where entrants ride a motorcycle a minimum of 1,000 miles in 24 hours or less. But I have ridden well over 100,000 miles over years of owning five Harley-Davidsons.

I've ridden across Montana prairies with the sun scorching down on me at 115 degrees for the entire day. I've been caught in early snowstorms in Utah not knowing if a tire would catch a patch of ice and I would find myself sliding into oncoming traffic or if I would make it to my destination without a mishap.

The scariest ride I ever had was riding in the middle of the night toward the northern Oregon coast and getting caught in a sudden and thunderous rainstorm. White-knuckled, I crouched behind my windshield while the rain pounded down on me and right into my boots and soaked me to the bone. To add to the misery, passing cars sprayed sheets of icy water onto me and the lights of oncoming traffic blurred in blinding intervals.

There was nowhere to pull off and wait it out. I had to keep going. So, I focused on the red taillights of the motorcycles ahead of me, gripped the bars tighter, and looked for milestones to shoot for: mile marker 291, the dim lights of a small, closed gas station ahead, the distant thought of a hot tub awaiting me at the motel in Astoria. Anything to keep my mind off my freezing body and chattering teeth.

I was determined to make it. Alive. And I did. It was a tough, arduous journey, but I made it. I kept my butt in the saddle and I rode to the finish line.

Being an entrepreneur feels just like that at times, but you ride it out. You keep going. You grip your goals tighter, focus on the milestones, and take it a mile at a time. You keep the checkered flag of your finish line in mind and keep riding until you get there.

FAILURE IS AN OPTION... QUITTING IS NOT

Everyone knows the famous Thomas Edison story. Though he was often ridiculed, Edison made more than 10,000 attempts before finally demonstrating the world's first working light bulb in 1879. When asked by a reporter, "How did it feel to fail 10,000 times?" Edison simply replied, "I didn't fail 10,000 times. The light bulb was an invention with 10,000 steps."

Thomas Edison invented the long-lasting light bulb, the phonograph, and the motion picture camera through extensive trial and error.

Another quote attributed to Edison reflecting his try, try again mindset:

"Success is 1 percent inspiration and 99 percent perspiration."

Without failing now and again, or finding a lot of ways that don't work, you will never learn how to become a better businessperson, how to develop a better product, or how to find the path that truly speaks to your purpose. Sure, the feeling of failure stings in the moment, but nothing feels better than getting back up and going for it again.

The biggest thing to consider is this: what did you learn?

When you fail, reevaluate your business plan, what you've done so far, and see what you need to change, add, or get rid of. Remember your *Why*? It will get you through these tough times.

Above all else, keep your eyes on the prize.

SACRIFICE, ORGANIZATION, DETERMINATION

Good habits are a great thing. Here are a few to cultivate if you're intent on getting your idea from concept to commercialization:

Sacrifice

They say, "If you want something you've never had, you have to do something you've never done." If your old or current habits haven't helped you reach your goal yet, they're not going to in the future. Start waking up earlier (or staying up later if you are the nocturnal type), go to fewer social events, watch less TV, consume less junk (mind and body). Your habits determine your future and by changing the ones that hold you back, you'll get closer to the finish line.

Organization

In today's digital age, there's absolutely no reason why you shouldn't keep a digital calendar; that way, it's always with you to keep you on track. You can also easily create voice memos and reminders to stay on track with your goals and responsibilities.

I use my Apple watch — it vibrates all day long with reminders, alarms, and timers. I also talk all day to Siri and Alexa. Use them all, or whatever works for you, to stay on track for the day, by the project, by the hour. You'll be amazed at how much more you accomplish and how much you remember to do if you utilize these tech tools.

When you're racing toward the finish line, excuses like, "I forgot" or "I didn't have time" aren't going to cut it. Scheduling out your days in an organized and easy-to-manage way will help you to reach your goals faster. Reminders will keep you on track.

Consistency

This is arguably the most important factor in attaining your goals — and possibly the hardest. I know that waking up at the same time every morning and going through the motions of implementing your business plan can be tough. In fact, it can become downright boooooorrrring to do the same thing every day at the same time, the same way, with the same people. So, change it up, but be consistent in doing what you have to do every day.

For example, instead of waking up to the obnoxious blaring shrill of your alarm, change it to oceans gently swishing against a white, sandy beach somewhere in the Caribbean, or a song you love to hear over and over. As a teenager, my mother used to blast John Philip Sousa's "Stars and Stripes Forever" into my room to wake me up. I hated it, but I did get up. Do what works for you, but get up. Get going. Get your stuff done.

Consistency builds trust within your team, with your customers, and with yourself. If you know you can rely on yourself to show up every day ready to give it 100 percent, everyone else will know it, too. It's contagious.

"Successful people aren't born that way. They become successful by establishing the habit of doing things unsuccessful people don't like to do."
— William Makepeace Thackeray

IT'S NOT ABOUT THE BIKE

RAGBRAI is an acronym and registered trademark for the Register's Annual Great Bicycle Ride Across Iowa, which is a noncompetitive bicycle ride organized by *The Des Moines Register*.

The ride crosses Iowa from west to east and draws recreational riders from all over the United States and many foreign countries. First held in 1973, RAGBRAI is the largest bike-touring event in the world.

Riders begin at a community on Iowa's western border and ride to a community on the eastern border, stopping in towns across the state. The ride is one week long, ending on the last Saturday of July each year, after beginning on the previous Sunday.

In one of my impulsive, insane moments, I decided I was going to ride this event, all 500-plus miles, which included the optional century loop (100 miles in one day). I had ridden in a couple of century rides before; how hard could another 400-plus miles be?

An overview of the 2011 route looked like this:

Day 1	Glenwood to Atlantic	59.5 miles
Day 2	Atlantic to Carroll	65.4 miles
Day 3	Carroll to Boone	70.9 miles + Karras Loop of 28.3
Day 4	Boone to Altoona	56.1 miles
Day 5	Altoona to Grinnell	57.5 miles
Day 6	Grinnell to Coralville	74.9 miles
Day 7	Coralville to Davenport	65.6 miles

I was able to join the most prestigious RAGBRAI team — Team Gourmet — as my talented niece Maggie Amerpohl was the head chef. Yes, the food every day was truly gourmet. The menu was printed on the front of our biking jerseys, and inevitably other riders passing us on the road would ask us daily, "What's for dinner tonight?" I would point to the front of my jersey as I passed them and reiterate our upcoming, amazing feast. At 6:00 p.m. every night we were the envy of the RAGBRAI tour.

The year I rode RAGBRAI XXXIX there were more than 25,000 riders and the temperatures across Iowa got as high as 97 degrees. I quickly learned I had to get up early, like in the F's—between four and five a.m. — to get a jump on the day, beat the crowds, beat the hot, sweltering, sweaty sun, and pace myself so I could reach my destination somewhere between sundown and total exhaustion.

Although I was spent at the end of each day, I had paced myself to each overnight town successfully. I had sacrificed sleeping in, avoided staying too long in the shade as I passed through each small and inviting town, and kept a steady, manageable pace. It worked.

Some of my team members didn't fare so well. They partied hard at night, went to all of the local bars on the way through each town, and then had to ride like crazy to get to our nightly camp by dinnertime. Many of these riders took a "day off," meaning they rode with the food truck to the next town that day instead of pedaling like the rest of us. Obviously, you can ride RAGBRAI any way you want, but in my mind, if you want to say you REALLY rode RAGBRAI, then you ride every day and finish every mile.

I organized my riding and my mindset into small chunks to be completed along the way: ride from starting point Atlantic, IA to Brayton. Brayton to Exira. Exira to Audubon. Audubon to Templeton. Templeton to Carroll.

I was consistent in my routine every day and paced myself to each day's finish line by completing A to B over and over. It's a marathon, not a sprint. I was able to complete the 500-plus mile ride, not because I trained better or I was in better shape or I had a better bike (it's not about the bike), but because I avoided burnout. I intentionally paced myself to finish well.

Avoiding Burnout

Your journey from mind to market will more than likely be a long one and something requiring perseverance and determination. However, if you spend every waking moment working, it's doubtful you'll be able to reap the fruits of your labor, because you'll be just too worn out.

To avoid burnout while racing toward the finish line, follow these rules of the road:

Stop at the Pit Stops

I used to despise my alarm clock. Truly. It was real hate. Being blasted out of a restful, dreamy sleep was the bane of my existence. I would be crabby for hours. My kids knew not to ask for anything that mattered for at least two hours.

Now, before it starts *beep beep beeping*, I am already out of bed and moving energetically about my sunrise-filled life.

One of the reasons is because I'm paying attention to my body's *circadian rhythm* — a 24-hour cycle that, regardless of morning alarms and evening appointments, my body is naturally inclined to follow.

This is one of the many things I learned when reading *Why We Sleep* by Matthew Walker, Ph.D.[26] We all need sleep — uninterrupted seven-to-eight-hours-a-night sleep. Dr. Thomas Roth, of the Henry Ford Hospital in Detroit, stated, "The number of people who can survive on five hours of sleep or less without impairment, and rounded to a whole number, is zero."

Walker claims that sleep produces complex neurochemical baths that improve our brains in various ways. And it "restocks the armory of our immune system, helping fight malignancy, preventing infection, and warding off all manner of sickness." In other words, sleep greatly enhances our evolutionary fitness — just in ways we can't see.

KEY TAKEAWAY: With too little sleep, we risk ill health and dangerous lapses of concentration. To live healthy, productive lives, we should listen closely to our body's internal clock, which tells us when, and how much, to sleep.
To learn more about the dangers of sleep deprivation, watch the interview with Dr. Matthew Walker on YouTube.

Why We Sleep

Running a new business isn't school, where you have to pull an all-nighter for a final the next day. Pace yourself, stop at the rest stops, take occasional breaks, and get the sleep you need to be at your best; you'll be more productive, do better work, and be more alert in the saddle.

When you've reached a major business goal, think about going on a well-earned weekend trip somewhere relaxing. You deserve it, and you'll be better at work the following week.

Draft Whenever Possible

One of the biggest benefits of riding in a biking group versus riding alone is the benefit of drafting. Drafting occurs when a cyclist moves into an area of low pressure behind another cyclist, reducing the wind resistance and the amount of energy required to pedal. During the ride, everyone in the group experiences the benefits of drafting by rotating the lead rider to the back of the paceline. If you do this correctly, the amount of effort you're putting in can be reduced by 30 percent, so you can go farther and faster.

Car racers draft, too. As a race car moves around the track, it splits the air, some going over the car and some beneath. This lack of air behind the car creates a vacuum, which a trailing car may use to be pulled or "towed."

In the business world, you can "draft" off of your team and therefore go further and faster. Letting qualified team members take the lead on specific projects not only saves you energy and time but also instills trust and team morale. Put your saved "30 percent" into things only you can do. Then when it's your turn to be in the lead again, you can gear up, and as the ultimate bicycle movie *Premium Rush* exhorts us, "Ride like hell."

Finish the Race

The only way to get to the finish line and commercialize your product is to never give up. Make sacrifices, stay organized, and be consistent. Keep in mind that taking little breaks along the way to avoid burnout is just as important as your persistence in accomplishing your business goals. Take care of your mind and body so you can keep going and going until the checkered flag is waving in your face.

Embrace Winston Churchill's motto: "Never give up on something that you can't go a day without thinking about."

Don't Drop the Ball at the One Yard Line

If you want to watch a series of videos that will make your stomach churn and your legs wobble, search "Celebrating Too Early" on YouTube. The miracle of the internet will provide you with a series of recorded instances of an athlete about to cross the "finish line" and began celebrating a supposed win.

You probably know what happens next. The ill-fated moment of premature celebration leads to the ultimate demise. For example, a competitor takes advantage of that hubris and sneaks ahead and crosses the finish line first, leaving the erstwhile leader in shame on the silver-medal podium.

What was once a moment of triumph for an elite athlete turns into a nightmare in a matter of milliseconds. The same tragic outcome can happen to even the most prepared and successful entrepreneurs — and often at the worst possible moment.

Cross. The. Finish. Line.

As you near the finish line and see the checkered flags waving wildly, it's imperative you don't drop the ball or ease up at the last minute to begin celebrating. You know the path you have taken to get to the final stage of the process. Now make sure you get there. Keep going at full throttle!

In business and product development, situations can change at a moment's notice. Outcomes that were clear and on the horizon at the start suddenly shift as a manufacturer goes under, an investor pulls out, or unforeseeable market conditions hit. Before you buy the celebratory champagne and balloons, make sure you have covered all the important factors of finalizing your idea.

If you have read all the episodes of *I Didn't See It Coming*, you are well aware of the horror stories that can unfold even for those with the most incredible ideas. I can't promise these won't happen to you. In fact, I'd be more comfortable betting money on the chance that you *will* have a few of those setbacks.

But it's okay. It's likely you have already run into unexpected issues and obstacles and have found creative ways to overcome them. Just remember, don't panic, and hold firm to what you have learned and put into practice so far.

You've stayed steady and consistent throughout the entire process up to this point, so hang on just a bit longer to ensure all of your loose ends are tied up. Even when you can see you have successfully brought your idea to market and are beginning to pocket a profit, keep pushing ahead.

When the moment comes when you can let loose and start truly celebrating, it will be easy to recognize. The market will know. Your team will know. Investors will know.

You will know.

CHAPTER 16 - Action Accelerators

THINK IT → ORGANIZE IT → DO IT

Take action on these items NOW to keep driving your idea from Brain to Bank:

1. Refer to your *Why*, and then write down five reasons why you will never give up on getting your project from brain to bank.

   1) ____

   2) ____

   3) ____

   4) ____

   5) ____

2. Write down how you will avoid burnout.

   ____

   ____

   ____

3. Take a look at three habits that keep a successful business owner in the game: sacrifice, organization, and consistency:

- Sacrifice: Name three ways you will sacrifice time, money, and/or physical labor to become successful in your new business.

  ____

  ____

  ____

- Organization: Name three ways you could be more organized. How will you integrate these new organizational improvements?

- Consistency: Name three inconsistencies you see in your business and/or your actions. What will you do to change them? How? When?

4. Now implement your solutions into your daily/weekly/monthly practices and watch the finish line move closer and closer.

5. Update your roadmap so it has the most current information.

STICK TO THE PLAN

Chapter 17

Victory Lap

GOING WITH THE FLOW

I literally grew up on the river. As the founder of one of the largest river-running companies in North America, my father, Jack Currey, started Western River Expeditions, still one of the finest and largest outfitters and providers of white-water adventures for over 62 years.

One of the first things my father instructed me on while preparing me for my first river trip at age eight was what to do if the boat flipped and I found myself in the water:

- **Number One:** Don't panic! You will float, you have on a life jacket. Life. Jacket. If you can swim to the boat, swim to the boat, and then hang on to the ropes strung along either side. Someone will pull you in. If the boat is upside down, you still need to stay with the boat.

- **Number Two:** If you are too far downstream past the boat, keep your feet downstream at all times. This will allow you to use your feet to bounce off rocks, canyon walls, and large tree branches lodged in the river. You'll also have a "downstream view" of what's coming up so you can dodge obstacles. At some point, you'll spot a place where you can swim to shore.

- **Number Three:** If you are in the middle of the rapids, you will most likely get sucked underwater, but this is temporary. You will soon be spewed up to the surface, and this is where you remember to take a breath in case you go underwater again. Remember rule number one: don't panic!

- **Number Four:** Go with the current. In a fast-moving environment like a whitewater river, don't attempt to swim upstream, even if you see a beach where you think you can crawl out. Swimming against the current will get you nowhere, wear you out, and keep you from getting to the safety of the shore downstream. Go with the current.

After running rivers for more than 50 years, I had never been in a flipped boat... not until I ran the Zambezi River in Zimbabwe. This was another part of the same African tour I took with my sister in 2007, and the much-anticipated river trip was to be its last adventure and crowning glory.

The first half of the river trip was filled with Class 4 and 5 white-water rapids, just what we'd signed up for — it was exhilarating! Even the crocodiles sunning along the banks seem to enjoy the screams of delight coming from each raft as it was engulfed in the tumultuous waters.

But sometime after our lunch break, our Zambezi River guide decided the trip thus far had not been as exciting as promised, and that all of his charges needed a "real story" to tell. In the next Class 5 rapid he abruptly turned his oar crosswise and purposely flipped our boat.

My sister and I had never found ourselves suddenly in the icy cold waters of a treacherous river... not to mention one that had crocodiles in it.

The words of our father came flooding back. We grabbed the ropes of our overturned boat, and then searched for a rescue kayak.

We did what we had learned to do decades ago. We didn't panic. We kept our feet downstream until we each located a kayak and then wrapped our arms and legs up around the front of it to keep the crocodiles from having one for lunch until we reached another boat that pulled us in.

But others in our boat who had no river experience panicked and had difficulty remembering what the guide had told them before we launched onto the river.

Everyone was rescued and no one was seriously hurt. But the panic they'd experienced stayed with them for the rest of the trip.

Just as a whitewater rafter may be flipped into a wild river without warning, you will have times when you find yourself upside down, disoriented, and submerged in an icy, cold plunge of business turbulence.

The same rules apply:

- **One:** Don't panic.
- **Two:** Keep your eyes on the prize downstream.
- **Three:** Take a breath when you can and think clearly about what to do next.
- **Four:** Don't waste your energy fighting upstream in unwinnable battles. Look downriver, go with the current of what's working, and land on a shore to regroup.

You'll find a nice "beach" to camp on for the night, dry off, wake up the next morning to a glorious sunrise, and set out to conquer the new day.

Take a victory lap reveling in the fact that you made it this far. Raise your hands high up into the air and yell, "Waaaaaaah hooooooo!"

Celebrate the small wins! Go crazy on the big ones!

You're on an adventure. Expect an upset or two. Don't panic. Remember the rules of the river.

And go with the flow.

RIDE BABY, RIDE!

As an entrepreneur, every day I embrace the words of Helen Keller:

"Life is a daring adventure... or nothing at all."

Taking your idea from Brain to Bank is just that... an adventure.

It's like riding through Class 5 rapids on a primitive South American river that's seldom been run.

It's like riding in an IndyCar at 230 miles an hour and taking the rubber-burning turns at full speed.

It's like riding a bicycle through a redwood forest as the sun rises through a lifting fog and the smell of the damp early-morning air mingles with a woodsy scent emanating from every tree.

It's like riding your motorcycle on the most challenging road in the Black Hills of South Dakota, better known as Iron Mountain Road, and navigating the hairpin turns one after another. The thunder-rumble of your pipes as they echo in the three tunnels along the route ends with a picturesque profile look at George Washington's head carved into the side of the Mount Rushmore as you emerge from the darkness.

It's like whatever that one thing is that gets you leaping out of bed early in the morning to get a jump on the day because you simply can't wait another minute to push your dream forward.

What's your daring adventure?

Whatever your dream ride is as an entrepreneur,
you're in for the ride of your life!

Think it.

Organize it.

Do it.

As the thrill-ride attendants buckle you in, they are famed for saying:

"Sit down. Hold on.
Keep your arms and legs in at all times.
And enjoy the ride!"

Appendix

Flow Chart for FDA-Approved Product

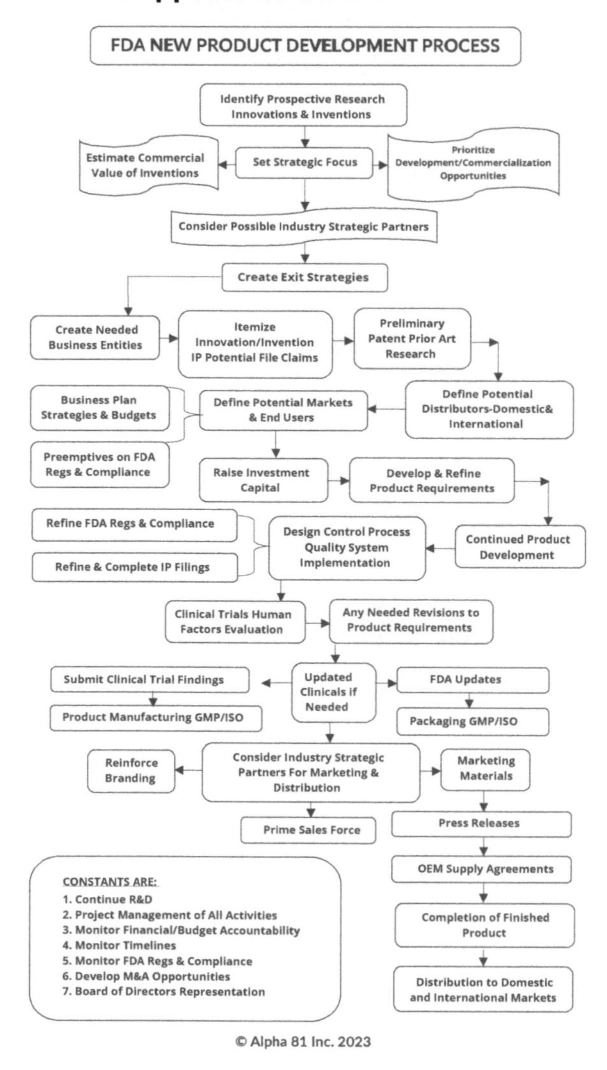

You can download this roadmap here: www.BrainToBank.com/Resources.

CRAFTING YOUR CUSTOMER AVATAR

Customer Avatar

- ✓ Buyer Persona
- ✓ Marketing Persona
- ✓ Customer Avatar
- ✓ Target Market

These are the phrases used interchangeably to describe the fictional, generalized representations of the persona most likely to buy from you.

It is critically important to the success of your marketing, sales, product development, and delivery of services that you have a deep understanding of who your Customer Avatar is. You've likely heard the phrase, "You can't hit a target you haven't set"; this applies beautifully to the importance of having a clearly defined Customer Avatar.

Having a deep understanding of a clearly defined Customer Avatar will help you:

- Determine what social platforms they are spending their time on so you know where your business should be present and active.

- Be more effective in your advertising. Your marketing dollars will be well spent when you know where to advertise and whom to target to maximize your exposure.

- Better connect with your Avatar through your copy because you will have an understanding of their pains, pleasures, desires, and wants.

- Deliver and develop better products/services because you are able to anticipate your market's needs, behaviors, and concerns.

Sample Dossier

Meet Sally the solopreneur

Age: 35+
Status: Married
Location: Arizona
Gross earnings: (cap E) $100k
Time in business: (cap B) 1yr +

Sally is a solopreneur who is age 35 or older and has been in business for one year or more. Sally works alone and runs all parts of her business.

Sally has a passion for serving others and loves what she does, but she is starting to see that her dreams of freedom, flexibility, and control are getting pushed farther out each day. She loves the fact that she owns her own business and that she does have some flexibility, but she feels like her business owns and controls her (instead of the other way around).

Sally is successful enough that she is earning close to $100k a year, but she is starting to find herself spending less time doing what she loves and more time dealing with the business side of her business. Sally is at the point where she is overwhelmed by the day-to-day activities of running the business — yet she wants to grow. Her business is no longer rewarding because she is doing things that she is not good at.

Her vision is to become an entrepreneur with the intention to grow her business by hiring a team that can do the things she isn't good at and doesn't want to do and also by automating the mundane tasks in her business that are important but suck up a lot of her time.

She is ready to take on the role of marketing as her full focus. Sally is keenly aware that marketing and systems are the keys to taking her business to the next level. Her focus is on growing revenue, creating systems, and positioning her business to scale. By implementing these strategies, she will create the cash flow in her business that she needs to hire and add stability.

Avatar Demographics

Geographic	
Age	
Generation (i.e. Baby Boomer, Millennial)	
Relationship status	
Education	
Work (i.e. employers, job title, schools)	
Income	
Home type (i.e. homeowner, renter)	
Other	

Avatar Interests

Business and industry (architecture, banking, business, construction, design)	
Entertainment (games, events, movies, music, reading, TV)	
Family and Relationships (dating, family, fatherhood, marriage, motherhood, parenting, weddings)	
Fitness and Wellness (bodybuilding, dieting, gyms, meditation, nutrition, physical exercise)	
Food and Drink (alcoholic beverages, cooking, food, restaurants)	
Hobbies and Activities (arts and music, home and garden, pets, travel, politics, vehicles)	
Sports	
Other	

Avatar Behaviors

Charitable donations	
Digital activities (gamers, Facebook admins, online spenders, small business owners, technology early adopters, late adopters)	
Financial (insurance, investments)	
Spending (credit card users, bank cards, retail stores, premium cards	
Purchase Behavior (kids' products, pet products, garden products, clothing)	
Travel	
Other	

Avatar General

What are their concerns related to your product/service?	
What has happened in the past that led them to this point?	
How do they feel about what happened in the past?	
What about your product/ service matters to this person?	
How does it solve a need, ease or eliminate pain, or make them feel good?	
How does it better their life?	
What goes through their mind before they purchase your product/service?	
What is the "final straw" that makes them pull the trigger and move forward with your product/service?	
Other	

You can download this worksheet here: www.BrainToBank.com/Resources.

Acknowledgments

As Robert Redford once expressed to the woman who rescued his oldest daughter from drowning in her submerged Bronco in a freezing river, "Thanks isn't enough." But let me at least name names in an attempt to immortalize the incredible individuals who are lifelong friends, esteemed colleagues, mentors, coaches, and supreme examples of innovative entrepreneurs who were successful in getting their ideas from brain to bank and gave of their time, knowledge, and heart to support and improve this book.

Thanks a million to my editors Jane Halsey and Carol Cartaino. I am once again reminded why authors thank their editors profusely. For without them, we are grammar error–ridden writers who sometimes don't know our homonyms from homophones from homographs. So we authors *accept* their corrections *except* when we don't due to stubbornness. For the nonedited, there might be more mistakes in *their* sentences because *they're* in dire need of editors. Your expertise in all of this is because *you're* the best. Did I get all of these homophones right?

The word "thanks" will never be enough for my lifelong friend Donna Tallman. Your attention to detail and command of sentence composition, flow, and continuity is well... nerdy, and of course, responsible for the improvements that added much-needed clarification and polish to this book. You are an amazing writer in your own right and I am lucky to learn from you.

To my creative friend Richard Hartley for his generous giving of time and expertise. As a multi-talented professor extraordinaire, your perception and comprehension of this book are uncanny, and I thank you for every minute you spent reading it and each suggestion you offered. Our working together started with our project "Meals on Wheels" for our master's degrees waaaaaay back when, and life has been better ever since.

Acknowledgment goes to Brad Bartlett, who offered suggestions for additional content that culminated in a greater understanding of and resources for each chapter.

Cheers to my New Mexico buddy and connoisseur of great books Brian Schroeder, whose quick wit, intellect, and inherent magnet-like attention to detail picked up on improvements that enhanced the overall reading and learning experience.

To Phil Chang I say Xièxiè 谢谢. As a seasoned digital marketer, content strategist, podcaster, and speaker in Ontario, Canada, Phil has long honed the skill of making a person feel as if they can do anything. His continuous smile is captivating, his enthusiasm contagious. Thanks for your time, your expertise, and your willingness to do whatever it takes to make things happen. Superheroes have nothing on you.

Thanks to the talented digital marketing expert Alexandra Cavadas. Her gracious giving of time and talent are only superseded by the warmth and generosity she gives to all.

Lots of "waahoos" and whitewater splashes to my river-running buddy Paul Mortensen for his uncanny and invaluable attention to detail. Because excellence is in the details, your edits made the book so much better.

Other valuable insights, suggestions, and corrections were given by my colleagues, friends, and family, who took the time to read an unpolished script and possessed the eagle-eye vision to grasp its concepts, stories, and, most importantly… yes, the jokes, which is why they have been paramount in my life for years.

Gratitude goes out to Ray Kurzweil of Kurzweil Technologies for graciously allowing me to use his Second Half explanation and graph on exponential technologies in Chapter 1 – Know Your Why. Ray Kurzweil is one of the world's leading inventors, thinkers, and futurists, with a 30-year track record of accurate predictions. Called "the restless genius" by *The Wall Street Journal* and "the ultimate thinking machine" by *Forbes* magazine, Kurzweil was selected as one of the top entrepreneurs by *Inc.* magazine, which described him as the "rightful heir to Thomas Edison." PBS selected him as one of the "sixteen revolutionaries who made America." I'm lucky to have connected with you.

Thanks to my friend and colleague John Cabrera in Bogotá, Colombia. He is an exceptional project manager, planner, action-plan executor, and all-around spectacular team player. His contributions to Chapter 2 – Mapping Out Your Action Plan – and the ClickUp template exceeded all expectations. The value you added to this book is priceless.

The collaborative efforts and generosity of Anthony Taylor in Chapter 3 – Paving Your Strategic Plan – made it possible to offer the best advice on a tough subject. Anthony founded SME Strategy Consulting in 2011 to help organizations and their people create and implement their strategic plans by facilitating strategic planning meetings, leading corporate training, and providing executive coaching and expert advice to senior leaders. Thank you for your willingness to share your vast knowledge and resources.

To the good people at LivePlan.com, I will forever be indebted to you for providing a simple, doable approach for Chapter 5 – Writing Your Business Plan. Whether an entrepreneur chooses the long or the short of it, you're there to make it easy. Thanks for sharing and playing well with others.

To Tim, Lonny, Flo, Adriana, and all those at Certified Financial Institute (CFI) who helped create and share the easy-to-understand information in Chapter 6 – Financials, Budgets, and Valium. Thank you! Your contributions made my life much easier, as I am still trying to figure out how to ride a bicycle like a fish.

Thanks to Jim Afinowich of IBG/Fox & Fin, a nationally respected, award-winning leader in business sales and acquisitions of privately held middle-market companies in every major industry. Chapter 8 – Create Exit Strategies – is better because of you. Jim's business acumen is uncanny, and he openly and readily shared his knowledge of M&A to help others succeed. He literally soars with the eagles. He has held advanced ratings for ultra-light aircraft and hang gliders, as well as conventional aircraft.

Terry Ludlow is the Founder, Chairman, and Chief Executive Officer (CEO) of Chipworks. In June of 2016 TechInsights and Chipworks announced the combination of their businesses, creating a global leader in advanced technology intelligence and technology-founded patent advisory services. Terry is a recognized leader and pioneer in the use of advanced semiconductor reverse engineering processes to support innovative product design and to extract maximum value from Intellectual Property (IP). His current company, Pachira, located in Ottawa, Canada, was founded as a contract patent licensing company that leveraged Chipworks technology knowledge for SME patent owner clients. Thanks, Terry, for contributing your infinite wisdom on the tough topic of Chapter 9 – Patents and Intellectual Property.

Paul Oestreich is an IP attorney at EminentIP, a full-service intellectual property law firm located in Salt Lake City. A friend and business colleague, he generously took time out of his busy schedule to read, edit, and contribute to Chapter 9 – Patents and Intellectual Property.

Brian Burt is a brilliant, seasoned, Harvard Law School–educated corporate attorney with the Snell & Wilmer law firm in Arizona. He is an extraordinary attorney and a good friend. Brian teaches a monthly seminar designed to educate entrepreneurs on various topics that will help them succeed. Thanks, Brian, for your willingness to share your wisdom and your contributions to Chapter 10 – Show Me the Money.

To the brilliant folks at East West Manufacturing, many thanks for sharing your proficiency in the detailed and precise world of DFM in Chapter 11 – Design for Manufacturability. Your capable company and employees demonstrated how to solve problems of the greatest magnitude for entrepreneurs and inventors in design, manufacturing, and distribution, and this knowledge helps us all to provide better products and increased value for our customers.

Thanks to my longtime friend and business colleague Shem Fischer for imparting his knowledge on manufacturing, his innate business savvy, and his continued encouragement for my projects.

To the genius Misty Kortes, I salute your creativity and marketing prowess. Without you, my avatar in Chapter 12 – Your Ideal Customer – would truly live in a futuristic jungle with large, pointy ears and glowing eyes. Instead, you made it easy to visualize and describe the perfect and ideal customer avatar. *I see you.* Thank you.

Thanks to the full-service digital marketing agency WebFX for sharing 13 buzzwords as part of Chapter 14 – Marketing to the Masses. It's apparent that your team made up of award-winning marketers, designers, and developers knows what it takes to get real results online. We're all more equipped to speak the lingo and walk the talk thanks to you.

Many calories of thanks to my incredibly talented niece Chef Margaret (Maggie) Amerpohl, who agreed to share her culinary genius by feeding our biking team five-star meals and allowing me to give the world her 2011 RAGBRAI menu in Chapter 16 – Crossing the Finish Line. Get it here:

www.BrainToBank.com/Resources.

Bon appétit!

NOTES

[1] For simplicity in navigating this book, the word "product" includes products and services.

[2] A relatively conservative estimate from Harvard Business School professor Clayton Christensen.

[3] Sinek, Simon. *Start with Why: How Great Leaders Inspire Everyone to Take Action.* Portfolio/Penguin, 2011.

[4] Used with permission. Ray Kurzweil, Kurzweil Technologies.

[5] Used with permission. Ray Kurzweil, Kurzweil Technologies.

[6] ClickUp is a cloud-based collaboration and project management tool suitable for businesses of all sizes and industries. Features include communication and collaboration tools, task assignments and statuses, alerts, and a task toolbar. The activity stream displays tasks as they're created and completed in real time. Built for teams from 1 to 1,000+.

[7] Used with permission. Anthony Taylor SME Strategy Consulting, Vancouver, B.C., Canada.

[8] Used with permission. Wakeam, Jason. "The Five Factors of a Strategic Alliance," *Ivey Business Journal*, May/June 2.

[9] Used with permission. Palo Alto Software. LivePlan.

[10] Used with permission. Palo Alto Software. LivePlan.

[11] Used with permission. Palo Alto Software. LivePlan.

[12] Financial professionals who want to work in investment banking are required by the Financial Industry Regulatory Authority (FINRA) to pass the Series 79 exam. Candidates must be sponsored by a FINRA member to take the exam. The exam covers topics like debt and equity offerings, mergers and acquisitions, and financial restructuring.

[13] The burn rate is the pace at which a new company is running through its start-up capital ahead of generating any positive cash flow. The burn rate is typically calculated in terms of the amount of cash the company is spending per month.

[14] Used with permission. Corporate Finance Institute.

[15] Sullivan, Dan and Hardy, Dr. Benjamin. *Who Not How: The Shift in Mindset That Will Help You Unlock Your Maximum Potential.* Hay House, Inc., 2020.

[16] As a disclaimer, please know that the purpose of the following information is to provide you with information on this topic, and nothing here should be construed as creating, offering, or memorializing the existence of an attorney-client relationship. The content should not be considered legal advice or opinion because the content may not apply to the specific facts of a particular matter or you or your project or your company. Alpha 81 does not provide legal advice. All information and materials are for educational purposes only. All parties are strongly encouraged to consult with their attorneys.

[17] Used with permission. TechInsights.

[18] Used with permission. TechInsights.

[19] Used with permission. LenPenzo.com.

[20] ©2009-2020 Brian J. Burt, Snell & Wilmer L.L.P. Such information may not be reproduced, in whole or in part, without the prior written consent of Mr. Burt in each instance.

[21] Dilution is when a company issues additional shares of stock, and it reduces the value of the existing investors' shares and their proportional ownership within the company.

[22] Used with permission. East West Manufacturing, LLC.

[23] Used with permission. Misty Kortes.

[24] Used with permission. www.WebFX.com.

[25] A/B testing is also known as split testing. It is a randomized experiment consisting of two or more versions of a variable such as a web page, page element, marketing ad, etc. that are shown to different segments of website visitors at the same time to determine which version leaves the maximum impact and drives business metrics.

[26] Walker, Matthew. *Why We Sleep: Unlocking the Power of Sleep and Dreams.* Scribner, 2017.

GLOSSARY

3PL
3PL stands for Third-Party Logistics. A 3PL is a company that provides a variety of outsourcing services related to the logistics and supply chain management of goods. The services offered by a 3PL can include transportation, warehousing, inventory management, and order fulfillment, among others.

3PLs are often used by companies to outsource certain logistics and supply chain management functions, allowing them to focus on their core business activities. By using a 3PL, companies can benefit from the expertise, resources, and economies of scale that the 3PL can provide. Additionally, 3PLs can help companies reduce costs, improve operational efficiency, and increase flexibility in their supply chain management.

A/B Market Test
A/B testing is a method of comparing two versions of a product or marketing campaign to determine which performs better. In an A/B test, two variants of a product or campaign (A and B) are randomly shown to two separate groups of users, and their behavior is compared to determine which variant performs better. This test is commonly used in web design, marketing, and product development to determine the best approach for a given situation. A/B testing allows for data-driven decision making, as it provides statistically significant insights into which version is preferred by the target audience. The results of an A/B test can then be used to inform future design or marketing decisions.

Accruals
Accruals refer to the recognition of revenue or expenses in accounting records before cash is received or paid. It refers to the adjustment of accounts to reflect financial transactions that have been recorded on the books but have not yet been settled in cash. Accruals help to match revenue and expenses to the period in which they were incurred, regardless of when payment is received or made.

Agile Project Management
Agile Project Management is a project management approach that prioritizes flexibility and collaboration. It is based on the Agile Manifesto, a set of values and principles for software development that emphasize customer satisfaction, adaptive planning, and delivering working software incrementally.

In Agile Project Management, a project is broken down into smaller, iterative cycles or sprints, allowing for continuous improvement and adaptation to changes in customer requirements or technology. This approach values face-to-face communication, regular retrospectives, and a focus on delivering value to the customer over strict adherence to a plan. Teams use agile techniques such as Scrum or Kanban to manage their work and prioritize tasks.

The Agile Project Management approach is commonly used in software development but has been adopted in other industries as well. It is particularly well suited to projects where requirements are uncertain, subject to change, or where a high degree of collaboration is required.

Angel Investor

An angel investor is a high-net-worth individual who provides capital to early-stage startups in exchange for equity or ownership in the company. Angel investors are usually experienced entrepreneurs or businesspeople who are looking for high-risk, high-reward investments.

Angel investors typically invest their own personal funds, as opposed to institutional funds, and often provide not only financial support but also mentorship, business expertise, and valuable industry contacts. They are often the first source of funding for startups that are too young to receive venture capital and are not yet profitable enough to secure a loan from a bank.

Angel investments are typically made in exchange for equity in the company, meaning that the angel investor becomes a partial owner of the company and is entitled to a portion of the profits if the company is successful. The amount of equity that the angel investor receives is typically negotiated between the investor and the startup.

Angel investing is a key source of funding for early-stage startups, and angel investors play an important role in helping young companies to grow and develop. By providing not only financial support but also business expertise, mentorship, and valuable industry contacts, angel investors can help startups to succeed and achieve their goals.

Article That Can Be Manufactured

An article that can be manufactured in the context of patents refers to a category of inventions that involve the creation of a new and unique physical product, such as a machine, apparatus, device, or other manufactured item. This category of patents encompasses a broad range of physical inventions, including consumer goods, electrical and mechanical devices, medical devices, and other tangible items.

To be eligible for an "article that can be manufactured" patent, the inventor must demonstrate that the claimed invention is new, useful, and non-obvious, and that the claimed invention provides a new and unexpected result compared to the prior art. Additionally, the inventor must provide a detailed description of the article and how it is manufactured and must provide drawings or other illustrations that clearly show the structure and function of the invention.

Avatar

A customer avatar, also known as a buyer persona, is a fictional representation of a company's ideal customer. It is a detailed profile of the customer, including demographic information, and their goals, challenges, behaviors, and values.

Creating a customer avatar helps companies understand their target audience and develop marketing and sales strategies that are more likely to resonate with them. By understanding their ideal customer, companies can create messaging that is more relevant, effective, and appealing to their target audience.

A customer avatar should include information such as the customer's age, gender, education level, income, job title, and geographic location. It should also include information about the customer's interests, motivations, pain points, and the benefits they are looking for from the company's products or services.

Developing a customer avatar is an important part of the marketing and sales process, as it helps companies to better understand their target audience and create messaging that is more likely to capture their interest. By focusing their efforts on their ideal customer, companies can maximize their marketing and sales efforts, reduce waste, and increase their overall return on investment.

Backend Metadata

Backend metadata refers to data that is stored in a backend system but is not directly visible to the end user. This type of metadata is used to support the functionality of the system or application, but it is not part of the actual content or presentation of the system.

Backend metadata can include information such as user accounts, system configuration data, access control lists, and other administrative data. It is used by the system to manage and control the flow of information and to ensure that the system is functioning properly.

Examples of backend metadata include the creation and modification dates of files and records, the user who created or last modified a file, and the permissions that are associated with a file or folder. This information is stored in the system's database or file system. It is not directly visible to the end user, but it is used by the system to manage and control the flow of information and to ensure that the system is functioning properly.

Backend metadata is important for maintaining the integrity and functionality of the system and for ensuring that information is properly managed and controlled. It plays a critical role in the overall design and implementation of the system and is essential for ensuring that the system is able to meet the needs of its users.

Backend System

The backend system refers to the server-side components of a web application, which are responsible for storing, processing, and serving data to the frontend (i.e., client-side) components. Backend systems can be built using various programming languages and technologies, such as Python, Java, Ruby, PHP, and Node.js. They typically communicate with the frontend through APIs (Application Programming Interfaces). The backend system is responsible for tasks such as managing databases, executing business logic, and providing security and scalability to the application.

Beta Tester

A beta tester is a person who tests a product or service before its official release to the public. Beta testing is the final stage of testing before a product or service is commercially released, and it is designed to identify any remaining bugs, issues, or problems with the product.

Beta testers are usually a representative sample of the target audience and are selected based on their experience, technical expertise, and ability to provide feedback. They are typically given access to a beta version of the product and asked to test it in real-world conditions and provide feedback on its performance, user experience, and overall functionality.

Boolean Search

Boolean search is a method for searching information that uses a combination of keywords and what are called "operators," such as AND, OR, NOT, and parentheses, to refine search results and find exactly what you are looking for. Boolean search is named after George Boole, the 19th-century mathematician who first formulated the concept of Boolean logic.

Boolean search allows you to combine keywords and operators to create complex search queries that can help you find more relevant information. For example, using the operator "AND" will return only results that contain both keywords, while using the operator "OR" will return results that contain either keyword. The operator "NOT" can be used to exclude certain terms from the search results.

Boolean search is commonly used in many online search engines, databases, and other information retrieval systems to provide more accurate and relevant results. It is especially useful when searching for information on a specific topic or when trying to find information that meets specific criteria. By using Boolean search, you can more effectively find the information you need and avoid irrelevant or unhelpful results.

Burn Rate

Burn rate refers to the rate at which a company is spending its available capital or cash reserves. It is typically expressed as the monthly or annual rate at which a company's cash balance decreases over time. Burn rate is an important metric for startups and early-stage companies, as it provides insight into the company's financial sustainability and the pace at which it is using its available resources.

For startups and early-stage companies, the burn rate is often used to gauge the company's financial health and to help determine the amount of funding that may be needed in order to reach profitability or reach a certain milestone. A high burn rate may indicate that a company is spending too much too quickly and may need to slow down its spending in order to preserve its cash reserves.

It is important to note that burn rate should be considered in conjunction with other financial metrics, such as revenue growth, customer acquisition costs, and gross margins, in order to gain a complete picture of a company's financial health and sustainability.

Business Accelerator

A business accelerator is a program designed to help early-stage startups grow quickly and efficiently. It provides mentorship, networking opportunities, access to funding and resources, and education and training to participating companies. The goal of a business accelerator is to help startups move from concept to market as quickly as possible and to increase their chances of success.

Unlike a business, which provides long-term support and resources, an accelerator program typically runs for a set period of time, such as 3-6 months, and culminates in a demo day or pitch event where startups present their businesses to potential investors. Business accelerators often focus on specific industries or types of technology, and they may take an equity stake in participating companies in exchange for their support.

Business Incubator

A business is a program or facility designed to support the development and growth of early-stage startups and small businesses. It provides resources, mentorship, and support services to entrepreneurs in order to help them turn their ideas into successful businesses. These resources can include office space, shared equipment, access to funding and investors, business training and education, and networking opportunities. The goal of a business is to increase the success rate and speed of growth for its participating businesses, and to foster a supportive ecosystem for entrepreneurship.

Business Plan Event

A Business Plan Event, also known as a business plan competition, is an event where entrepreneurs or startups present their business plans to a panel of judges, investors, or other industry experts. The goal of a Business Plan Event is to provide a platform for entrepreneurs to showcase their ideas, network with potential investors and partners, and receive feedback and advice from experienced industry professionals.

In a Business Plan Event, participants typically present their business plans in a formal setting and may be asked to answer questions or provide additional information about their products, services, or business models. The judges or panelists then evaluate the business plans and select winners based on criteria such as the strength of the business idea, the feasibility of the business plan, and the potential for future growth and success.

Business Plan Events are often organized by business s, accelerators, venture capital firms, or universities, and they may offer prizes or awards to the winners, such as funding, mentorship, or office space. They provide a valuable opportunity for entrepreneurs to gain exposure, build their network, and receive valuable feedback and advice to help them grow their businesses.

C Corporation

A C Corporation, or C Corp, is a type of business structure that is taxed as a separate entity from its owners. C Corps are the traditional type of corporation and are recognized as a separate legal entity from its owners, known as shareholders. The profits of a C Corp are taxed at the corporate level, and then again when they are distributed to the shareholders as dividends. C Corps can have an unlimited number of shareholders, can issue stocks, and can raise capital through the sale of stocks. They also offer liability protection to their shareholders, as the shareholders' personal assets are generally protected from the company's debts and liabilities. However, the double taxation of C Corps can make them a less attractive option for some businesses compared to other structures such as S Corps or LLCs.

Call Option

Calls and puts are types of option contracts in finance. An option is a financial instrument that gives the holder the right, but not the obligation, to buy or sell an underlying asset, such as a stock, at a specified price within a specified time period.

A call option gives the holder the right to buy the underlying asset at a specified price, known as the strike price (which see), within a specified time period. If the price of the underlying asset increases above the strike price, the holder of the call option may exercise the option and buy the underlying asset at the lower strike price, realizing a profit.

Options trading can be complex and involve a significant amount of risk, and it is important for individuals to have a thorough understanding of the market and the underlying assets before engaging in options trading. Options can be used for various purposes, such as hedging against potential losses, generating income, or speculating on price movements.

Churn

"Churn" in investing refers to the frequent buying and selling of securities within a short period of time, often resulting in a high level of transaction costs and taxes. Churn is typically associated with high-frequency trading, where investors buy and sell securities multiple times in a day, or even in the same day, in an attempt to profit from short-term price fluctuations.

Churning can be a problem for individual investors because it can result in high transaction costs, such as brokerage fees and taxes, that can eat into any profits earned. Additionally, frequent buying and selling can also increase the risk of market timing errors, where an investor buys or sells a security at the wrong time and misses out on potential profits.

Churning is generally discouraged by investment advisors and financial experts, who suggest that individual investors take a long-term approach to investing and avoid frequent buying and selling of securities. Instead, they recommend a well-diversified investment portfolio, held for the long term, as the best way to build wealth over time and minimize investment risk.

Click-Through Rate (CTR)
Click-through rate (CTR) is a measure of the effectiveness of online advertising. CTR is the ratio of clicks on a specific ad to the number of impressions (or times the ad was displayed) for that ad. CTR is usually expressed as a percentage, and it provides a quick way to measure the engagement and performance of an ad.

For example, if an ad is displayed 100 times and receives 10 clicks, the CTR for that ad would be 10%. A higher CTR indicates that the ad is more engaging and relevant to the target audience, and is therefore more likely to drive conversions or sales.

CTR is a key metric used by advertisers and marketers to assess the effectiveness of their online advertising campaigns. By tracking CTR, they can optimize their ad copy, targeting, and placement to improve the performance of their ads and achieve better results. CTR is also used by publishers and online platforms to determine the relevance and value of an ad and set pricing for advertising slots on their sites.

ClickUp (Software/App)
ClickUp is a cloud-based productivity and project management platform that provides a wide range of tools for organizing and managing tasks, projects, and teams. ClickUp offers features for task management, time tracking, goal setting, and team collaboration, among others. Some of the key features of ClickUp include:

- Task Management: Creating and managing tasks, setting deadlines, and tracking progress.
- Time Tracking: Tracking time spent on tasks and projects and generating detailed reports.
- Goal Setting: Setting and tracking personal and team goals, and monitoring progress towards achieving them.
- Team Collaboration: Sharing tasks, communicating with team members, and working together on projects.
- Integration: Integrating with other tools and apps, such as Google Drive, Slack, and Trello.

ClickUp aims to provide a centralized platform for managing work and productivity, and to make it easier for individuals and teams to collaborate and get work done more efficiently. The platform is designed to be user-friendly and customizable, and it offers a range of pricing plans to meet the needs of different users and teams.

Collateral-Trust Certificate
A collateral-trust certificate is a type of investment instrument that is backed by a specific asset or collateral. The asset serves as a guarantee for the repayment of the investment, giving the investor a certain level of security and protection.

Collateral-trust certificates are often used in the context of debt securities, where the assets backing the investment serve as collateral for the debt. This means that if the borrower is unable to repay the debt, the assets can be sold to repay the investor. This helps to reduce the risk of default, making the investment more secure.

The specific assets that back the investment can vary, but they often include real estate, vehicles, equipment, or other types of tangible assets. The terms of the collateral-trust certificate, such as the interest rate, the maturity date, and the repayment terms, are typically negotiated between the issuer and the investor.

Collateral-trust certificates are a type of structured finance product, and they can provide a way for investors to access a specific asset class or to gain exposure to a particular market or sector. However, they can also be complex and may carry higher risks than other types of investments, so it's important to understand the terms and conditions of the investment before investing.

Commercial Simulation Packages
Commercial simulation packages are simulation software tools that are sold commercially and are typically developed by for-profit companies. These packages usually come with advanced features, technical support, and regular updates, but they often also come with a high cost and licensing fees. Examples of commercial simulation packages include ANSYS, COMSOL Multiphysics, and MATLAB.

Composition of Matter
Composition of matter in the context of patents refers to a category of inventions that involve a new and unique combination of chemical elements or molecules, or a new chemical formula, which gives rise to a novel and non-obvious product or substance. This category of patents encompasses a broad range of chemical innovations, including new drugs, polymers, catalysts, fuels, and other chemical substances, as well as modifications to the structure of existing compounds. To be eligible for a composition of matter patent, the inventor must demonstrate that the claimed invention is new, useful, and non-obvious, and that the claimed invention provides a new and unexpected result compared to the prior art.

Content Curation
Content curation is the process of selecting, organizing, and presenting content from multiple sources to a specific audience. The purpose of content curation is to provide value to the audience by presenting them with relevant and high-quality content that is carefully selected and organized by a trusted expert or organization. This can be done in many different formats, including blog posts, social media posts, newsletters, or web pages.

Content curators play a critical role in the modern media landscape by sifting through vast amounts of content to find and present only the most relevant and valuable information to their audience. Content curation requires a deep understanding of the target audience, a broad knowledge of the topic being covered, and the ability to evaluate and select only the best content for inclusion.

Examples of content curation can be found in many areas, including news, technology, fashion, and music, among others. By providing a trusted and reliable source of information, content curation can help to build a loyal following, establish expertise, and provide value to the target audience.

Content Management Services
Content Management Services (CMS) refer to a set of tools and technologies used to create, manage, and publish digital content, such as websites, blogs, and online applications. A CMS typically includes a user-friendly interface that allows non-technical users to create and publish content without the need for technical knowledge or programming skills. Some common features of a CMS include:

- Content creation and editing tools
- Version control for tracking changes to content
- Workflow management for coordinating the approval and publication of content

- Search engine optimization (SEO) tools to improve visibility and search ranking
- Integration with other systems, such as marketing automation and analytics platforms

The goal of a CMS is to make it easier for organizations to create and publish digital content, and to provide a centralized location for storing and organizing that content. By using a CMS, organizations can improve the efficiency and accuracy of their content production, and ensure that their content remains up-to-date and accessible to users.

Contract Research Organization (CRO)

A Contract Research Organization (CRO) is a third-party service provider that specializes in offering research and development services to pharmaceutical, biotechnology, and medical device companies. CROs provide a range of services, including preclinical research, clinical trials, regulatory affairs, and laboratory services, among others. The goal of CROs is to provide support and expertise to companies, enabling them to focus on their core activities while outsourcing non-core activities to a specialist provider.

CROs help companies to reduce the cost and time involved in bringing new products to market, by providing access to specialized expertise, facilities, and technology. CROs are regulated by government agencies and must comply with strict quality standards, including Good Clinical Practice (GCP) and Good Laboratory Practice (GLP), among others. The use of CROs has become increasingly common in the pharmaceutical and biotechnology industries, as companies look to outsource non-core activities and reduce the risk and cost of drug development.

Controlled Technical Dictionary

A Controlled Technical Dictionary (CTD) is a type of specialized technical glossary that is used to ensure consistency and accuracy in the use of technical terms and definitions within an organization. The CTD is usually maintained by a central authority, such as a technical writing department or a standards committee, and is used as a reference source for all technical documents produced within the organization. The CTD contains definitions of terms that are commonly used in the organization's technical field, and it is updated regularly to reflect changes in technology or terminology. The use of a CTD helps to ensure that technical information is communicated accurately and consistently across different documents, projects, and departments, and reduces the risk of misunderstandings or misinterpretations.

Conversions

Online conversions refer to the completion of a desired action by a user on a website or online platform. A conversion occurs when a user takes a specific, desired action, such as making a purchase, signing up for a newsletter, downloading an app, filling out a form, or making a phone call.

Online conversions are important for businesses because they represent a successful outcome of their marketing and sales efforts. By tracking conversions, businesses can measure the effectiveness of their online campaigns and websites and make data-driven decisions to improve their results.

Measuring and optimizing online conversions is an important part of digital marketing and website optimization. By using tools such as website analytics, A/B testing, and conversion rate optimization, businesses can make data-driven decisions to improve the user experience, increase the number of conversions, and achieve better business results.

Core Technology

Core technology refers to the fundamental and critical components of a product, service, or system that gives it its unique and essential characteristics. It is the underlying technology that makes a product work and distinguishes it from its competitors. Core technology is often protected by patents, trademarks, or copyrights, and it is considered a key asset of a company. The term can refer to a wide range of technologies, including software, hardware, engineering processes, and materials science, depending on the industry and context. Companies often invest significant resources into developing, refining, and protecting their core technology in order to maintain a competitive advantage and ensure long-term growth and success.

Cost of Goods (COGS)
Cost of Goods Sold (COGS) is a term used in accounting and finance to refer to the direct cost associated with producing a product or service. COGS includes all the direct costs involved in producing a product, such as raw materials, direct labor, and manufacturing overhead. COGS does not include indirect costs, such as marketing, research and development, and general administrative expenses.

COGS is an important metric for businesses, as it provides a measure of the cost of producing and selling a product. By knowing the COGS, a company can calculate its gross profit, which is the amount by which its revenue exceeds its COGS. Gross profit is a key performance indicator that provides insight into a company's profitability, and can be used to make decisions about pricing, production, and investment. COGS can also be used to compare the cost of producing products across different time periods, and to identify trends in the cost of goods sold.

Cross-Selling
Cross-selling is a sales technique in which a seller promotes or suggests additional products or services to a customer who is already interested in purchasing something. The goal of cross-selling is to increase the value of each sale by encouraging the customer to purchase complementary or supplementary products or services, or to upgrade to a higher-end product. Cross-selling can be done in various forms, such as in-person sales, phone sales, email marketing, or online recommendations. For example, a customer who is buying a new laptop may be offered an extended warranty, a laptop case, or an antivirus software. Cross-selling can be a win-win situation for both the customer and the seller as it can increase the customer's satisfaction with their purchase and boost the seller's revenue.

Custom Audience Pixel
A Custom Audience Pixel is a small piece of code provided by Facebook that is used to track website visitors and create targeted advertising campaigns on the social media platform. The pixel is placed on a website, and it collects data on the behavior of website visitors, including the pages they visit, the products they view, and the actions they take. This data is then used to build a "Custom Audience" of people who have interacted with the website.

This Custom Audience can then be targeted with advertising campaigns, such as Facebook ads, to drive traffic and conversions. The Custom Audience Pixel is a powerful tool for online marketers, as it allows them to reach people who have already shown an interest in their products or services. By targeting these people with highly relevant and personalized advertising, companies can improve the efficiency and effectiveness of their marketing campaigns and increase the likelihood of converting website visitors into customers. The Custom Audience Pixel is a feature of the Facebook Ads platform, and it can be used by businesses of all sizes to build and target Custom Audiences.

Data Visualization
Data visualization is the process of converting raw data into graphical or pictorial representations, such as charts, graphs, maps, and images, with the goal of making it easier to understand and analyze the data. The visual representation of data helps to identify trends, patterns, and insights that would be difficult to detect in raw data form.

Data visualization is used in many fields, including business, science, and engineering, to communicate data-driven insights and support decision-making. There are many different types of data visualizations, including bar charts, line charts, scatter plots, histograms, pie charts, heat maps, and more, each with its own strengths and best uses. The selection of the appropriate visualization depends on the type of data, the message to be conveyed, and the audience being addressed. With the growing amount of data being generated, the use of data visualization has become increasingly important in understanding and utilizing data.

Design Control Process
Design control process is a systematic approach used to manage the development and release of new products, services, or systems. It is a key component of a quality management system and is used to ensure that new products or systems meet the needs and requirements of stakeholders, such as customers, regulators, and end-users.

The design control process helps to ensure that new products or systems are developed and released in a controlled and consistent manner, and that they meet the needs and requirements of stakeholders. This helps to reduce the risk of problems or defects, and to increase customer satisfaction and confidence in the product or system.

Design for Manufacturing
Design for Manufacturing (DFM) is an approach to product design that focuses on optimizing the manufacturing process, cost, and quality of a product. The goal of DFM is to design products that are easy and cost-effective to manufacture, while still meeting all functional and performance requirements. The idea behind DFM is to minimize the number of manufacturing operations required to produce a product, reduce the cost of raw materials, and minimize waste, while maintaining the desired product quality. To achieve this, DFM takes into account factors such as material selection, part geometry, tooling, and assembly methods, among others. By implementing DFM principles early in the design process, manufacturers can reduce production costs, improve efficiency, and increase the speed of getting products to market.

Dilution
Dilution refers to the reduction in the ownership percentage, value, or voting power of a stock or share as a result of the issuance of new shares. In the context of equity financing, dilution occurs when a company issues new shares to raise capital, thereby increasing the number of outstanding shares and decreasing the ownership percentage of existing shareholders. This can result in a decrease in the per-share value of the stock and a reduction in the voting power of existing shareholders. Dilution can also occur as a result of stock-based compensation plans, such as stock options, which add new shares to the company's outstanding stock.

Earned Media
Earned media refers to publicity or exposure that a brand or organization receives through media coverage, word of mouth, or social media mentions that are not directly paid for by the company. This type of media coverage is earned as a result of the brand's actions, reputation, or message, and is considered more credible and trustworthy than paid or

owned media. Examples of earned media include news articles, customer reviews, and social media posts that mention a brand or product.

Elevator Pitch

An elevator pitch is a brief, persuasive speech that a person or company can use to spark interest in what you or your organization does. It's called an elevator pitch because it should be short enough to deliver in the time it takes for an elevator ride, typically about 30 seconds to 2 minutes. The goal of an elevator pitch is to capture the listener's attention, convey key information about the product, idea, or project, and motivate them to take further action or ask for more information.

Empirical Relationship

An empirical relationship is a relationship or association between two or more variables that has been established through observation and experimentation. Empirical relationships are based on actual data and evidence and can be used to make predictions about future events or trends. Empirical relationships are often used in statistics, where they are used to model the relationship between variables and make predictions. The strength of the relationship between variables can be measured using statistical methods, such as correlation coefficients, which describe the degree to which changes in one variable are associated with changes in another.

Equity Position

Equity position refers to the ownership of a company's stock or assets by an individual or organization. In other words, an equity position represents a share in the ownership of a company and the right to share in its profits and assets. An equity position can be obtained through the purchase of stocks or other securities in the company, or through the contribution of assets or services in exchange for an ownership stake. For example, an individual who buys 100 shares of a company's stock has an equity position in that company and is entitled to a portion of its profits and assets.

Executive Summary

A brief overview of a business plan or proposal that highlights its main objectives, strategies, and financial projections. The purpose of an executive summary is to quickly and effectively communicate the most important information contained in the larger document. It should provide enough information to enable the reader to understand the purpose and potential of the project, the problem being addressed, the proposed solution, the expected outcomes, and the resources required.

Factoring

Factoring is a financial transaction and a type of debt financing in which a business sells its accounts receivable (invoices) to a third-party financial organization called a "factor" in exchange for immediate cash. The factor pays the business a portion of the value of the invoices upfront and collects payment from the customers on behalf of the business. Factoring can provide businesses with quick access to cash that they would otherwise have to wait to receive from customers. It can also help businesses manage their cash flow and mitigate the risk of non-payment by customers.

Finite Element Analysis (FEA)

FEA (Finite Element Analysis) is a numerical simulation technique used to analyze the behavior of structures and components under various loading conditions. FEA involves dividing the structure or component into smaller, manageable elements or "finite elements," and then applying mathematical algorithms to calculate the behavior of each element under various loads. The results are then combined to assess the overall behavior of the structure or component. FEA is used in a wide range of industries, including aerospace, automotive, civil engineering, and mechanical engineering, among others. The goal of FEA is to provide a virtual representation of the structure or component, which can be used to study its behavior, optimize design, and make informed decisions about the design and operation of the system. FEA can be used to analyze various types of loading conditions, including static, dynamic, and thermal loads, among others. The results of FEA can be used to identify areas where efficiency could be improved, design cycle time reduced, and development cost minimized, among other benefits.

Flow Simulation

Flow simulation is the computational modeling of fluid flow in a system. It involves the use of mathematical and computer algorithms to predict the behavior of fluid flow, including velocity, pressure, temperature, and turbulence, among other properties. Flow simulation is used in a wide range of industries, including aerospace, automotive, chemical, and energy, among others. The goal of flow simulation is to provide a virtual representation of the fluid flow, which can be used to study the behavior of the fluid, optimize design, and make informed decisions about the design and operation of the system. The results of flow simulation can be used to identify areas of improved efficiency, reduce design cycle time, and minimize development costs, among other benefits. Flow simulation can be performed using a variety of software tools, including commercial and open source simulation packages.

Fractional Undivided Interest

Fractional Undivided Interest (FUI) refers to a type of ownership structure where multiple parties hold a shared ownership interest in a single property or asset, such as real estate, drilling rights, or minerals. Under this structure, each owner holds a fractional, undivided interest in the property, which means they have an equal right to use, benefit from, and share in the profits or losses of the property.

For example, if an oil well is owned by 10 individuals, each with a 10% FUI, they would collectively own 100% of the well and would share in any profits or losses in proportion to their ownership interest. However, since the ownership is undivided, no single owner can sell or transfer their interest without the consent of the other owners.

Fractional undivided interests are commonly used in real estate investment trusts (REITs), limited partnerships, and other investment vehicles, and can provide individuals with access to investments that would otherwise be beyond their financial reach.

Funding Gap

A funding gap refers to the difference between the amount of financing required to implement a project or program and the amount that is currently available. It can occur in government, nonprofit, or business contexts and represents the additional funds needed to reach a specific goal or complete a project successfully. The funding gap is often an obstacle that must be overcome through fundraising, grants, loans, or other forms of financing.

Gantt Chart

A Gantt chart is a type of bar chart that represents a project schedule and shows the start and end dates of tasks, and the dependencies between them. It is commonly used in project management to visualize and track the progress of tasks over time and help identify any potential scheduling conflicts.

Grow a Business

Growing and scaling a business refers to the process of expanding a company's operations and increasing its revenue and market share. The goal of growing and scaling a business is to increase its impact, reach, and profitability.

To grow and scale a business, companies typically focus on several key areas:

- Customer Acquisition: Acquiring new customers and expanding the customer base through effective marketing and sales strategies.
- Product Development: Improving and expanding the product offerings to meet the evolving needs of customers.
- Operations: Streamlining processes and systems to increase efficiency, reduce costs, and support growth.
- Finance: Securing funding and managing financial resources to support growth and scale.
- Talent Management: Hiring and developing the right people to support the growth and scale of the business.

Growing and scaling a business can be challenging, but it is also a key factor in ensuring long-term success and stability. Companies must be strategic in their approach and prioritize their efforts to ensure sustainable growth.

Hypernym

A word or term that encompasses a group of related words or concepts, where the hypernym is more general than the related terms (also known as hyponyms). For example, flower is a hypernym for hibiscus, lily etc.

Hyponym

A hyponym is a word that refers to a specific type of a more general term, also known as a superordinate. For example, canine is a hyponym of animal.

Internet of Things (IoT)

The Internet of Things (IoT) refers to a network of physical devices, vehicles, home appliances, and other items that are embedded with sensors, software, and connectivity, allowing them to collect and exchange data over the internet. IoT devices can be connected to each other and to the internet, enabling them to communicate and interact with each other and with users, regardless of time and location. The purpose of IoT is to create a seamless and interconnected system of devices that can be controlled and monitored remotely, and that can improve efficiency, safety, and convenience in various industries and applications, such as smart homes, connected cars, industrial automation, and healthcare.

Investment Banking 79 License

The Investment Banking Series 79 exam, also known as the Limited Representative-Investment Banking (LR-IB) exam, is a license required for, individuals who wish to engage in investment banking activities, such as underwriting, securities offerings, and private placements. The Series 79 exam is administered by FINRA (Financial Industry Regulatory Authority) and tests the knowledge and understanding of candidates in areas such as securities laws, regulations, investment banking products and services, underwriting and distribution of securities, and ethical and professional standards. Successful completion of the Series 79 exam is a requirement for individuals who wish to become licensed as a limited representative-investment banking in the securities industry.

IPO (Initial Public Offering)
An Initial Public Offering (IPO) is the process by which a privately held company becomes publicly traded by offering shares of its stock to the public for the first time. This event usually occurs when a company wants to raise capital by issuing and selling shares of stock to a wide range of individual and institutional investors. Investors who purchase shares in an IPO become owners of a portion of the company and can benefit from its future growth and success.

ISO Manufacturing Standards
ISO (International Organization for Standardization) Manufacturing Standards are international standards that are used to improve the quality, safety, and efficiency of the manufacturing process. These standards provide a framework for manufacturers to ensure that their products are consistent, reliable, and meet customer expectations.

ISO Manufacturing Standards cover a wide range of topics, including product design, production processes, quality control, supply chain management, and environmental management. Some of the most commonly used ISO Manufacturing Standards include:

- ISO 9001: This standard specifies the requirements for a quality management system and is widely recognized as the benchmark for quality management systems.
- ISO 14001: This standard sets out the requirements for an effective environmental management system, designed to help organizations minimize their environmental impact.
- ISO 22000: This standard covers the food safety management system and outlines the requirements for the production, processing, packaging, and storage of food products.
- ISO 13485: This standard is specific to the medical device industry and outlines the requirements for quality management systems in the design, development, and production of medical devices.

Kanban
Kanban is a visual project management method used in software development and other fields, designed to help teams optimize their work processes and prioritize tasks based on their urgency and importance. It is based on the concept of a "Kanban board," a physical or virtual board with columns that represent different stages of a work process, and cards that represent individual tasks and their status. The aim of Kanban is to create a visual representation of workflow, promote continuous improvement, and limit work in progress to avoid overburdening team members.

Key Performance Indicators (KPI)
Key Performance Indicators (KPI) are metrics used to evaluate and measure the success of an organization's strategies, objectives, and goals. They are quantifiable measures that track progress and help to determine if an organization is on track to meet its targets. KPIs provide organizations with an accurate and concise picture of their performance and help to identify areas for improvement.

KPIs are specific, measurable, achievable, relevant, and time-bound (SMART) metrics that are selected based on the organization's strategic priorities. They can be related to various areas of the business such as financial performance, customer satisfaction, employee productivity, operational efficiency, and more. Organizations can track their KPIs over time to evaluate their progress, identify trends, and make informed decisions.

Examples of KPIs include customer satisfaction ratings, return on investment (ROI), cost per customer acquisition, employee turnover rate, and website traffic. By monitoring

KPIs, organizations can ensure that they are making progress towards their goals and can make adjustments to their strategies as needed.

Language Processing

Language processing is the field of study and technology concerned with the automated analysis, understanding, generation, and manipulation of human language. It involves various tasks such as text classification, sentiment analysis, named entity recognition, machine translation, and question-answering, among others. It is a subfield of artificial intelligence and computational linguistics and is critical for natural language processing (NLP) systems, which see. These systems are designed to enable computers to process and analyze large amounts of human language data and to interact with humans in a more natural and intuitive way. Applications of language processing can be found in areas such as voice-activated virtual assistants, chatbots, information retrieval, and sentiment analysis of social media data.

Limited Liability Company (LLC)

A Limited Liability Company (LLC) is a type of business structure that combines the liability protection of a corporation with the tax benefits and flexibility of a partnership. In an LLC, the owners, known as members, have limited personal liability for the debts and obligations of the business, meaning their personal assets are generally protected. The management and ownership structure of an LLC can be structured in various ways, making it a popular choice for small businesses and entrepreneurs.

Local Pack

Google's Local Pack is a feature that displays a list of relevant local businesses at the top of the search engine results page (SERP) for certain search queries. The Local Pack is designed to provide users with quick and easy access to information about local businesses, including their names, addresses, phone numbers, and customer ratings and reviews. When a user searches for a local business or service, such as "pizza restaurants near me," the Local Pack will display a map with the locations of nearby businesses, as well as a list of three to seven businesses that match the user's search criteria. The businesses displayed in the Local Pack are selected based on a number of factors, including their proximity to the user's location, their relevance to the user's search query, and their overall reputation and popularity, as determined by Google's algorithms.

Machine Learning (ML)

Machine learning (ML) is a subfield of artificial intelligence that focuses on the development of algorithms and statistical models that enable computers to "learn" from data, without being explicitly programmed to do so. Machine learning algorithms use patterns in data to make predictions or decisions, improving their accuracy over time as they are exposed to more data. There are different types of machine learning, including supervised learning, unsupervised learning, semi-supervised learning, and reinforcement learning. Machine learning has a wide range of applications, including image and speech recognition, natural language processing, recommendation systems, fraud detection, and predictive modeling, among others. It is one of the fastest growing and most impactful technologies in recent years, transforming industries and solving complex problems.

Matching Principle

The Matching Principle in accounting is an accounting concept that states that expenses must be recorded in the same period as the related revenues they help to generate. The principle requires companies to match their expenses with the revenues they generate in order to accurately reflect the financial performance of a business in a given period. This helps to provide a clearer picture of the company's financial health, as well as ensuring that financial statements are prepared in accordance with generally accepted accounting principles.

Metrics

Metrics refer to measurable values or indicators used to track and evaluate the performance or progress of a system, process, or activity. Metrics can be used to track virtually any aspect of a system or process, including financial performance, customer satisfaction, marketing effectiveness, and operational efficiency, among others.

In business and other organizations, metrics are commonly used to monitor progress against goals, assess the success of various initiatives, and make data-driven decisions. Effective metrics are specific, meaningful, and actionable, meaning that they accurately reflect the performance or progress being measured, are relevant to the goals of the organization, and can be used to inform decisions or drive changes.

Metrics can be quantitative or qualitative in nature, and can be represented in a variety of ways, including charts, graphs, and tables. Common examples of metrics include sales revenue, customer satisfaction scores, website traffic, and social media engagement.

Milestones

Milestones are defined points in time or specific achievements that mark the progress of a project, program, or objective. They are significant events or accomplishments that signal the completion of a major phase of work or the achievement of a key objective. Milestones are typically used to establish a timeline for a project or program, and serve as a way to measure progress and ensure that the project remains on track.

Milestones are usually assigned specific dates and may be accompanied by specific deliverables, such as completed tasks, draft reports, or finished products. In many cases, milestones serve as checkpoints that allow the project team to review progress and make any necessary adjustments to keep the project moving forward. Milestones are also used to communicate progress to stakeholders, including senior leadership, customers, and other project participants.

Examples of milestones include the completion of a critical task, the delivery of a major project component, the successful launch of a new product or service, or the completion of a phase of construction. Milestones are often critical to the success of a project and are used to ensure that projects are completed on time, within budget, and to the required quality standards.

Minimum Viable Product (MVP)

A Minimum Viable Product (MVP) is a version of a product with enough features to satisfy early adopters and provide feedback for future development. The MVP is typically used as a testing ground to validate the viability of a product idea before investing significant resources into full development. The MVP is designed to deliver just enough value to attract early customers, test the product's value proposition, and gather feedback to guide future development.

The MVP is often a simplified version of the final product and focuses on delivering the core features and functionalities that are critical to the product's success. It is not meant to be a complete product but rather a starting point from which to iteratively develop and improve the product over time.

By creating an MVP, startups and other companies can avoid wasting time and resources on developing a full product that may not be successful. Instead, the MVP allows for continuous feedback, iteration, and improvement based on real-world data and customer feedback. This approach helps companies move faster, minimize risk, and make better decisions on product development.

Mobile Optimization
Mobile optimization refers to the process of optimizing a website or web content to ensure it provides an optimal viewing and interaction experience on mobile devices, such as smartphones and tablets. This includes elements such as responsive design, fast load times, and user-friendly navigation, among others, to enhance the user experience and improve search engine rankings.

Natural Language Processing (NLP)
Natural Language Processing (NLP) is a field of computer science and artificial intelligence concerned with the interactions between computers and human (natural) languages. The goal of NLP is to develop algorithms and models that enable computers to analyze, understand, and generate human language. NLP techniques are used to process and analyze large amounts of textual data, such as news articles, social media posts, and customer reviews, to extract valuable insights and information.

NLP tasks include speech recognition, text classification, sentiment analysis, machine translation, named entity recognition, and text generation. NLP algorithms use techniques such as lexical analysis, parsing, semantic analysis, and pragmatics to understand and interpret the meaning of human language. NLP technologies are widely used in various applications, such as search engines, chatbots, and customer service automation, to enhance human-computer interaction and improve efficiency and accuracy.

NLP is a challenging field due to the complexity and ambiguity of natural languages, and it is an active area of research and development. Advances in NLP have the potential to revolutionize the way computers interact with humans and to unlock new opportunities in areas such as healthcare, education, and customer service.

Non-Disclosure Agreement (NDA)
A Non-Disclosure Agreement (NDA), also known as a Confidentiality Agreement, is a legally binding contract that restricts the sharing of confidential information between two parties. The purpose of an NDA is to protect the confidential information of one party from being disclosed to third parties without the owner's consent. The NDA outlines the types of information that are considered confidential, the responsibilities of each party to protect that information, and the consequences for breach of the agreement.

NDAs are commonly used in business and commercial relationships, such as in mergers and acquisitions, joint ventures, licensing agreements, and employment contracts. They are also used in the technology and software development industries to protect intellectual property and trade secrets. The NDA helps to ensure that confidential information is not disclosed, misused, or misappropriated, and provides a legal remedy in case of a breach of the agreement.

Open-Source Simulation Packages
Open-source simulation packages are simulation tools that are freely available and can be modified, distributed, and used by anyone. They are developed by a community of developers and users and are typically maintained through contributions and volunteer work. Open-source simulation packages are usually less sophisticated than commercial packages, but they offer a lower cost alternative and the ability to customize the code to

meet specific needs. Examples of open-source simulation packages include OpenFOAM, OpenSees, and FEniCS.

Operational Plan

An operational plan is a detailed plan that outlines the specific actions and resources necessary to achieve an organization's goals and objectives. It is a comprehensive guide for day-to-day operations and focuses on the processes, systems, and activities that are critical to delivering results. An operational plan covers the specific steps, tasks, and responsibilities of individuals and teams involved in executing the strategy and achieving the desired outcomes. It also outlines the resources needed, such as personnel, budget, technology, and materials, to achieve the goals of the organization.

Organic Growth

Organic growth in business refers to the growth of a company through increasing its sales and profits from existing products, services, and markets, rather than through mergers, acquisitions, or external funding.

Organic growth is often seen as a desirable form of growth for a business because it is achieved through the company's own efforts and resources, rather than relying on external factors. This means that the growth is sustainable and is based on a strong foundation of existing customer relationships, market share, and brand recognition.

Organic growth can be achieved through a variety of methods, including:

- Increasing sales to existing customers: This can be accomplished through cross-selling, up-selling, or improving the customer experience.
- Expanding into new geographic markets: This can be done by opening new locations or entering new countries or regions.
- Developing new products or services: This can be achieved through research and development, or by acquiring new technologies or intellectual property.
- Improving operational efficiency: This can be done by streamlining processes, reducing costs, or improving productivity.

Organic Search

Organic search refers to the process of finding and retrieving information from a search engine's index through a search query, where the results are ranked based on relevance and importance, rather than by paid advertising or other commercial considerations. Organic search results are the non-sponsored links that appear at the top and bottom of a search engine results page (SERP, which see) and are determined by the search engine's algorithm, which takes into account factors such as keywords, content relevance, and website quality and authority. The objective of organic search optimization is to improve a website's ranking in the organic search results in order to drive more organic traffic to the site.

Original Equipment Manufacturer (OEM)

An Original Equipment Manufacturer (OEM) is a company that produces products that are then rebranded and sold by another company under its own name. The OEM manufacturer provides the product design, manufacturing, and other related services, while the rebranding company provides the marketing, distribution, and customer support for the product.

OEM relationships are common in many industries, including electronics, automotive, and computer hardware, among others. The OEM model allows companies to outsource the production of certain components or products, allowing them to focus on their core business activities, such as marketing, distribution, and customer support. The OEM manufacturer benefits from the arrangement by being able to sell a large volume of products and increase its production capacity.

Pass-Through Taxation

Pass-through taxation is a tax system that applies to certain types of business entities, such as partnerships, limited liability companies (LLCs), and S corporations. In a pass-through tax system, the business itself does not pay federal income tax on its profits. Instead, the profits and losses of the business "pass through" to the owners, who report their share of the profits or losses on their individual tax returns. The owners are then responsible for paying federal income tax on their share of the business's profits.

The main advantage of pass-through taxation is that it allows business owners to avoid double taxation. With traditional C corporations, the business pays corporate income tax on its profits, and then the shareholders pay individual income tax on any dividends they receive from the corporation. With pass-through taxation, the business's profits are only taxed once, at the individual level.

Pass-through taxation can also offer certain tax benefits to business owners, such as the ability to deduct business expenses and losses on their individual tax returns. This can result in a lower overall tax bill for the business and its owners.

Patent Assertion Entity

A Patent Assertion Entity (PAE) is a company that acquires patents primarily for the purpose of enforcing them through licensing or litigation. PAEs, also known as "patent trolls," do not produce products or services themselves, but instead generate revenue by asserting their patent rights against other companies that they believe are infringing on their patents. They often target smaller companies that cannot afford to defend themselves in court, and demand licensing fees or settlements in exchange for not pursuing legal action. The practice of PAEs has been criticized for stifling innovation and creativity, and many efforts have been made to reform the patent system and reduce the impact of PAEs.

Patent Mining

Patent mining refers to the process of identifying and extracting valuable information from a large set of patent data. Patent mining can be used to gain insights into various aspects of the patent landscape, such as technological trends, market opportunities, and competitive intelligence. The process typically involves the analysis of large datasets of patent data using various techniques, including natural language processing, machine learning, and data visualization.

Patent mining can be used for a variety of purposes, including technology monitoring, competitive intelligence, market research, and licensing. For example, companies can use patent mining to identify trends in a specific technological area and assess the competitive landscape. Additionally, patent mining can help companies identify potential licensing opportunities by identifying patents that may be available for licensing or that may be relevant to their business.

Pre-Organization Certificate or Subscription

A pre-organization certificate or subscription refers to a written statement of intention to form a corporation or a company. It is a document that indicates the intention of individuals to incorporate a business and outlines the basic terms and conditions of the proposed corporation, such as the name, purpose, and initial capital structure. In some jurisdictions, filing a pre-organization certificate or subscription with the relevant government agency is a prerequisite for incorporating a business. It may also serve as evidence of the parties' agreement to form the corporation and can be used to solicit additional investors or raise capital.

Prior Art

Prior art in the context of patents refers to all information that has been publicly disclosed or made available to the public, including patents, published articles, public use, or sale, before the filing date of a patent application. The purpose of examining prior art is to determine the novelty and non-obviousness of an invention, as a key requirement for obtaining a patent is that the invention must be new and non-obvious in light of the prior art. If the claimed invention is found to be anticipated or obvious based on the prior art, the patent application may be rejected by the patent office.

Privilege on a Security

A privilege on a security is a special right or advantage granted to a specific group of individuals or entities, usually to help them achieve a specific financial or operational objective. In the context of securities, privileges may be granted to insiders, such as company executives, or to large investors, such as institutional investors, to help them make more informed investment decisions.

Privileged access to inside information, early access to initial public offerings (IPOs), or more favorable terms on debt offerings are examples of privileges that may be granted to select investors. These privileges are often intended to incentivize these individuals or entities to invest in the company, provide capital, or take other actions that support the success of the enterprise. However, privileges may also create conflicts of interest and raise concerns about fairness and equity, so they are subject to regulation and oversight.

Pro Forma

A pro forma is a term used to describe a financial document or statement that is presented on a projected or estimated basis, rather than actual results. Pro forma financial statements are often used in business and financial analysis to estimate the future performance of a company based on various assumptions, such as future sales, expenses, and capital expenditures.

Pro forma statements can be used for a variety of purposes, including projecting future financial performance, evaluating the impact of a proposed transaction or investment, or presenting a more favorable picture of a company's financial situation for investors or stakeholders. Pro forma statements are not audited or verified by an independent party and do not reflect actual results, so they should be considered as estimates rather than actual results.

Put Option

Puts and calls are types of option contracts in finance. An option is a financial instrument that gives the holder the right, but not the obligation, to buy or sell an underlying asset, such as a stock, at a specified price within a specified time period.

A put option gives the holder the right to sell the underlying asset at a specified price, known as the strike price, within a specified time period. If the price of the underlying asset decreases below the strike price, the holder of the put option may exercise the option and sell the underlying asset at the higher strike price, realizing a profit.

Options trading can be complex and involve a significant amount of risk, and it is important for individuals to have a thorough understanding of the market and the underlying assets before engaging in options trading. Options can be used for various purposes, such as hedging against potential losses, generating income, or speculating on price movements.

Quality Management System (QMS)
A Quality Management System (QMS) is a framework of policies, procedures, and processes that organizations use to ensure they meet customer and regulatory requirements while continuously improving their performance. It includes all aspects of a business' activities that contribute to the creation and delivery of products and services. Commonly referred to as Total Quality Management (TQM), a QMS aims to improve customer satisfaction and organizational efficiency by reducing errors, waste, and inconsistencies. Examples of widely used QMS standards are ISO 9001 and Six Sigma.

Read on the Target
"Read on the target" in the context of patents refers to a review or analysis of a patent application or issued patent that is focused on determining the extent to which the claimed invention meets the requirements for patentability. A "read on the target" analysis is often performed as part of a freedom-to-operate or validity study, to determine if a proposed product or process would infringe any existing patents. It is also performed in the context of patent litigation, to determine the validity and enforceability of a patent.

Rescission Rights
Rescission rights refer to the right of an investor to cancel a securities purchase and receive a full refund of the purchase price. This right usually must be exercised within a specific time frame after the purchase and is often granted to investors as a protection against fraud or material misstatements in the offering of the securities. Rescission rights are often provided for under federal securities laws, such as the Securities Act of 1933, and can also be included as a term in the offering document for the securities. They give investors the opportunity to reconsider their investment and, in some cases, to correct a mistake they made at the time of the purchase.

Return on Investment (ROI)
Return on Investment (ROI) is a financial metric used to evaluate the performance of an investment. It measures the amount of return on an investment relative to the investment's cost. The ROI formula is calculated by dividing the gain from an investment by the cost of the investment, and then multiplying the result by 100 to express it as a percentage. The higher the ROI, the more profitable the investment has been. ROI is used to compare the efficiency of different investments and to evaluate the success of a particular investment or project. It is an important metric for individuals and businesses as it provides a straightforward way to evaluate the performance of investments and helps to make informed decisions about allocating resources.

Roth IRA
A Roth IRA is a type of individual retirement account (IRA) that offers tax-free withdrawals in retirement. Unlike traditional IRAs, contributions to a Roth IRA are made with after-tax dollars, meaning that the contributions are not tax-deductible in the year they are made. However, qualified withdrawals from a Roth IRA in retirement are tax-free, and there are no required minimum distributions (RMDs) during the account holder's lifetime. The contribution limits for a Roth IRA are typically lower than for a traditional IRA and are subject to income restrictions. Contributions can be made to a Roth IRA at any age as long as the account holder has earned income, and there is no age limit for making contributions. The investment options for a Roth IRA are similar to those for a traditional IRA and can include stocks, bonds, mutual funds, and exchange-traded funds (ETFs). A Roth IRA can be a valuable tool for retirement savings, offering tax-free growth and withdrawals in retirement.

S Corporation
An S Corporation, or S Corp, is a type of corporation that has elected a special tax status with the Internal Revenue Service (IRS) under Subchapter S of the Internal Revenue Code. This allows the business to be taxed as a pass-through entity, meaning that the business itself is not taxed on its income. Instead, the profits and losses are passed through to the individual shareholders, who report this income on their personal tax returns. This allows the business to avoid double taxation, as only the shareholders are taxed, not the corporation. To be eligible for S Corp status, the corporation must meet certain requirements, such as being a domestic corporation, having no more than 100 shareholders, and having only allowable shareholders, among others.

SaaS Platform
SaaS stands for "Software as a Service." A SaaS platform is a software delivery model in which a software application is hosted by a third-party provider and made available to customers over the Internet. Customers access the software via a web browser or mobile app, and do not need to install or run the software on their own computers. SaaS platforms are typically subscription-based, with customers paying a monthly or yearly fee to use the software. Examples of SaaS platforms include customer relationship management (CRM) software, human resources (HR) software, and project management software. The SaaS model allows customers to access powerful software applications without the need for significant upfront investment in hardware or IT infrastructure.

Scale a Business
Growing and scaling a business refers to the process of expanding a company's operations and increasing its revenue and market share. The goal of growing and scaling a business is to increase its impact, reach, and profitability.

To grow and scale a business, companies typically focus on several key areas:

- Customer Acquisition: Acquiring new customers and expanding the customer base through effective marketing and sales strategies.
- Product Development: Improving and expanding the product offerings to meet the evolving needs of customers.
- Operations: Streamlining processes and systems to increase efficiency, reduce costs, and support growth.
- Finance: Securing funding and managing financial resources to support growth and scale.
- Talent Management: Hiring and developing the right people to support the growth and scale of the business.

Growing and scaling a business can be challenging, but it is also a key factor in ensuring long-term success and stability. Companies must be strategic in their approach and prioritize their efforts to ensure sustainable growth.

Scrum
Scrum is an Agile framework for managing and completing complex projects. It was originally developed for software development but has since been applied to a wide range of industries, including product development, marketing, and IT.

Scrum is based on the principles of transparency, inspection, and adaptation. The framework consists of a set of defined roles, events, and artifacts that work together to enable teams to deliver high-quality results in a collaborative and efficient manner.

Scrum has become a popular approach for managing complex projects due to its flexibility, transparency, and focus on delivering high-quality results. It has been widely adopted in organizations of all sizes and industries and has been proven to be effective in delivering high-quality products and solutions.

Search Engine Results Page (SERP)
A Search Engine Results Page (SERP) is the list of results that a search engine returns in response to a user's query. It displays websites, images, videos, and other content relevant to the user's search query. The SERP shows the ranking of each website based on various factors, such as relevance and authority, which are determined by the search engine's algorithm. The top results on a SERP are usually the most relevant and authoritative, and they tend to receive the most clicks. The layout of a SERP may vary, but it usually includes several ads and organic search results. The objective of search engine optimization (SEO) is to improve the ranking of a website on the SERP, making it more visible to users and increasing the chances of attracting more traffic to the site.

Self-Directed IRA
A Self-Directed Individual Retirement Account (IRA) is a type of retirement savings account that gives the account holder the ability to invest their retirement funds in alternative assets, such as real estate, private businesses, precious metals, and more. Unlike traditional IRAs, which are typically limited to stocks, bonds, and mutual funds, self-directed IRAs provide a wider range of investment options. The account holder has control over the investment decisions but must still comply with the rules and regulations set by the IRS regarding contributions, distributions, and prohibited transactions. Self-directed IRAs can be either a Traditional IRA or a Roth IRA and offer the potential for tax-advantaged investment growth. However, it's important to note that investing in alternative assets comes with greater risks and requires a higher level of knowledge and expertise compared to traditional investments.

Sentiment Analysis
Sentiment analysis is a natural language processing task that involves classifying the sentiment of a piece of text as positive, negative, or neutral. It is commonly used in various industries, such as marketing and customer service, to gather and analyze customer opinions and emotions towards products, services, and other entities. The goal of sentiment analysis is to determine the attitude or emotion of the author or speaker towards a particular topic or subject.

SI Metric Prefixes
SI Metric Prefixes are standardized prefixes used to indicate multiples or fractions of units in the International System of Units (SI). The prefixes are added to base units to express a larger or smaller quantity. The most common prefixes are kilo (k), mega (M), giga (G), milli (m), micro (μ), and nano (n). For example, "kilo" represents 1000 times the size of the base unit, so a kilometer is 1000 meters. "Milli" represents one-thousandth of the size of the base unit, so a milliliter is one-thousandth of a liter. The use of SI metric prefixes helps to simplify and standardize the expression of very large or very small values in scientific, technical, and engineering applications.

Six Sigma
Six Sigma is a data-driven quality management strategy that aims to improve the quality of a process by identifying and removing the causes of defects and minimizing variability in manufacturing and business processes. The goal of Six Sigma is to achieve a process that produces no more than 3.4 defects per million opportunities. It uses statistical

methods and a structured problem-solving approach to improve efficiency, reduce waste, and increase customer satisfaction.

Slide Deck
A slide deck is a set of slides that are typically used for presenting information or making a pitch in a visual format. A slide deck can contain a variety of media including text, images, charts, and videos. The slides are usually presented in a linear sequence, with the presenter advancing through the deck to highlight the most important points. The format is commonly used in business and academic settings, as well as in many other contexts.

Small Business Administration (SBA)
The Small Business Administration (SBA) is an independent agency of the federal government of the United States that provides support to small businesses. The SBA provides a range of services and programs, including access to financing, counseling, and training, and disaster assistance. One of its main functions is to guarantee loans made to small businesses by commercial lenders, which helps these businesses access capital they might not otherwise be able to obtain. The SBA also provides education and resources to help small business owners start, grow, and succeed. The agency's goal is to promote and strengthen the role of small businesses in the American economy and to help entrepreneurs and small business owners access the resources they need to succeed.

Small Business Innovation Research (SBIR)
The Small Business Innovation Research (SBIR) program is a competitive, merit-based program that provides federal research funding to small businesses to support the development of new, high-risk, high-reward technologies. The program is designed to stimulate technological innovation and to encourage small businesses to participate in the federal R&D arena. The SBIR program is administered by various federal agencies, including the National Science Foundation, the National Institutes of Health, and the Department of Defense.

To be eligible for SBIR funding, a small business must have fewer than 500 employees and be based in the United States. The program provides funding in two phases: the first phase provides seed funding for the development of a concept, while the second phase provides funding for further development and commercialization of the technology. The funding is provided through a competitive, merit-based process, with awards made to the most promising proposals.

The SBIR program is a valuable resource for small businesses that are engaged in research and development activities. It provides funding and resources that can help small businesses bring new products and services to market and contribute to the growth of the U.S. economy. The program is also a source of innovation for federal agencies, as the research funded through the SBIR program often leads to new technologies that can be used to address important national needs.

Small Business Transfer Research (STTR)
The Small Business Technology Transfer Research (STTR) program is a U.S. federal government program designed to support the transfer of innovative technologies from small businesses to the federal government. The program is jointly managed by the Small Business Administration (SBA) and several federal research agencies, including the National Science Foundation, the National Institutes of Health, and the Department of Defense.

The STTR program provides funding and technical assistance to small businesses that are engaged in research and development activities in partnership with a research institution. The program aims to encourage small businesses to commercialize their technology and bring new products and services to market. STTR awards are made through a competitive, merit-based process that evaluates the technical and commercial potential of the proposed technology.

The STTR program is open to small businesses that have fewer than 500 employees and are based in the United States. Participating small businesses are required to partner with a research institution, such as a university or government laboratory, to perform the research and development activities. The program provides a unique opportunity for small businesses to access funding and resources to help bring their innovative ideas to market and contribute to the growth of the U.S. economy.

Social Media Content Curation

Social media content curation is the process of finding, organizing, and sharing relevant and valuable content from various sources on social media platforms. It involves selecting content that aligns with a specific topic, theme, or audience, and then presenting it in a way that adds value and insights to followers. The goal of social media content curation is to provide a source of information and inspiration to followers while also establishing the curation account or individual as a thought leader in the industry.

Social media content curation can be done manually or through the use of curation tools and platforms. Effective content curation requires an understanding of the target audience and a keen eye for identifying high-quality content that resonates with them. The curated content can be in the form of text, images, videos, or any other format that is suitable for the specific social media platform. Content curation helps organizations and individuals to build their brand, engage with followers, and stay relevant in a fast-paced and constantly evolving digital landscape.

Social Shares

Social shares refer to the act of a user sharing content, such as a blog post, article, or video, with their social media network. Social shares can be accomplished through various means, such as clicking a share button on a website, copying and pasting a link into a social media post, or using a social media sharing plugin.

In the context of online marketing, social shares are an important metric because they can help to increase the reach and visibility of a piece of content. When a user shares a piece of content, their followers and friends are exposed to it, which can help to drive traffic to a website, increase brand awareness, and generate leads and sales.

In addition, social shares can be a powerful form of social proof, which is the idea that people are more likely to follow the actions of others, especially those in their network. When a piece of content is shared by a large number of people, it can increase its credibility and make it more appealing to others, leading to even more shares and increased reach.

Stand-Alone Technology

Stand-alone technology refers to a system, device, or piece of software that operates independently and is not connected to any other device, network, or system. Stand-alone technologies can be used on their own and do not require any additional hardware or software to function. For example, a stand-alone calculator is a self-contained device that can perform mathematical operations without the need for an external computer or internet connection. Similarly, a stand-alone software program can be installed and run on a single computer, without the need for any other software or network connection. Stand-alone technologies are typically simpler and easier to use than their networked or integrated counterparts, but they also offer less functionality and are not able to share data or resources with other devices.

Star or Proud Patent

The term "star patent" is used in the patent industry to refer to a patent that is considered to be particularly valuable or important due to its significance in a particular technology field or its potential for generating revenue through licensing or litigation. A star patent may be particularly strong in terms of its claims, its breadth of coverage, or its longevity, making it a key asset for the patent holder. In some cases, a star patent may be the cornerstone of a company's intellectual property portfolio, or a key component of its competitive advantage. In other cases, a star patent may be highly sought after by other companies or individuals, leading to licensing deals or patent disputes.

The value of a star patent is often determined by various factors, such as the market for the technology it covers, the strength and validity of the claims, and the level of competition in the field. The value of a star patent can change over time as technology evolves and as the patent landscape changes. Overall, a star patent is considered to be a valuable asset for the patent holder and is often a key factor in business and legal decisions related to intellectual property.

Straddle

A straddle is a type of options trading strategy that involves holding both a call option and a put option for the same underlying security, with the same strike price and expiration date. The goal is to profit from significant price movements in either direction, regardless of the direction of the price change. This strategy is often used when the investor expects a large price movement but is unsure of the direction of the move.

Strike Price

The strike price, also known as the exercise price, is a key component of options contracts in finance. The strike price is the predetermined price at which the holder of the option may buy (in the case of a call option) or sell (in the case of a put option) the underlying asset, such as a stock, within a specified time period.

The strike price is set at the time the option contract is purchased, and it is used as a benchmark for determining whether the option is in-the-money (ITM), at-the-money (ATM), or out-of-the-money (OTM). If the price of the underlying asset is higher than the strike price of a call option, the option is ITM and may be exercised for a profit. If the price of the underlying asset is lower than the strike price of a put option, the option is ITM and may be exercised for a profit. If the price of the underlying asset is equal to the strike price, the option is ATM. If the price of the underlying asset is not favorable for the option holder, the option is OTM and is likely to expire worthless.

The strike price is a critical component of options trading and is used to determine the potential profit or loss from an options contract. It is important for individuals to understand the strike price and its implications for the potential profit and loss of an options trade.

SWOT Analysis

SWOT analysis is a strategic planning tool used to evaluate the Strengths, Weaknesses, Opportunities, and Threats (SWOT) of a business or organization. It is a systematic approach to identifying internal and external factors that can impact the success of a project, business, or organization. The aim of a SWOT analysis is to understand the current situation and develop strategies that take advantage of opportunities, minimize weaknesses, and mitigate threats. The output of a SWOT analysis is commonly presented in a matrix format, with each factor placed into one of the four categories.

Thermoforming
Thermoforming is a manufacturing process used to produce plastic parts. A sheet of plastic is heated until it is pliable, and then placed over a mold or form. Then air pressure or a vacuum is used to form the plastic into the shape of the mold. The process involves heating a sheet of plastic to its forming temperature, placing it over a mold or form, and then using air pressure or vacuum to form the plastic into the shape of the mold. The plastic is then cooled and removed from the mold. Thermoforming is a versatile and cost-effective manufacturing method that is used to produce a wide range of plastic products, including packaging, trays, covers, and enclosures, among others. The process is well suited for producing large, complex parts with a high degree of dimensional accuracy, and can be used to produce parts in various materials, including polyethylene, polypropylene, and PVC, among others.

Unicorn
A "unicorn" in the context of investing refers to a privately held startup company that has a valuation of over $1 billion. The term was first popularized in the tech industry but has since been used to describe any company with this level of valuation regardless of industry. The term "unicorn" reflects the rarity of these companies, which are seen as having significant growth potential.

Up-Selling
Up-selling is a sales technique where a seller tries to convince a customer to purchase a more expensive item, upgrade, or add-on, by emphasizing its value and benefits over the original item the customer intended to buy. The goal of up-selling is to increase the sale value and profit for the seller.

Venture Capital Investor (VC)
A venture capital investor is a type of investor who provides capital to startups or early-stage companies with high growth potential. Venture capital investors typically invest in companies that are in the process of developing new products or services, and that have not yet established a track record of commercial success. The goal of venture capital investing is to generate high returns through equity ownership in the companies they invest in, as these companies grow and mature over time. Venture capital investors typically have a long-term investment horizon, and provide not only capital but also strategic and operational support to the companies they invest in. They typically invest in industries such as technology, biotechnology, and clean energy, among others.

Virtual Assistant (VA)
A virtual assistant (VA) is a type of software application or a human worker that provides administrative or personal assistance to users over the internet. Virtual assistants use artificial intelligence (AI) algorithms, natural language processing (NLP), and other technologies to understand and respond to users' requests. They can help with a variety of tasks, such as scheduling appointments, booking travel arrangements, managing emails, and providing information.

In the context of human virtual assistants, a virtual assistant is a professional who provides administrative, technical, or creative assistance to clients remotely from a home office or another location outside of the client's workplace. Virtual assistants are hired on a contract or freelance basis and perform tasks such as managing emails, booking appointments, conducting research, and preparing reports.

Both AI and human virtual assistants have become popular due to the rise of remote work and the need for more efficient and cost-effective administrative support.

Voting-Trust Certificate

A voting trust certificate is a type of security that represents ownership of a specific number of shares in a corporation and confers the right to vote those shares. The voting rights are transferred from the shareholder to a trustee for a specified period of time, usually 10 years. The purpose of a voting trust is to concentrate voting control in a small number of individuals or entities, making it easier to achieve a particular outcome in corporate decision making, such as a merger or change in management. Voting trusts are often used in cases where it is difficult to secure a controlling interest through direct ownership of shares.

Voice

Your "voice" in marketing refers to the unique tone, style, and messaging that a company or brand uses to communicate with its target audience. It's a reflection of the company's personality and values and helps to differentiate it from its competitors. A brand's voice should be consistent across all its marketing materials, from its website and social media to its advertisements and email campaigns. It should also align with the brand's overall strategy and target audience, as well as resonate with the emotions and needs of its customers. Having a distinct and authentic voice can help to build trust and establish a deeper connection with customers, leading to increased brand loyalty and long-term success.

Index

About the Author

Dorine Rivers, "River" to her friends, literally grew up on North and South American rivers rafting wild whitewater rapids, basking in the sun, and sleeping under a canopy of brilliant constellations. She transferred by osmosis her enthusiasm for the outdoors to her five children (all successful in their own right now) and her 20 grandchildren.

River has an undergraduate degree in creative writing, a Ph.D. in Business Management, Investment Banking and General Contractor licenses, and a few other degrees and certifications in between. She is the CEO of Alpha 81 Inc., an Arizona-based firm successfully supporting corporate innovations, expansions, and exits in software, technology, medical, life/health sciences, education, and other industries.

Her expertise is in strategic planning and management, and in building effective business infrastructures by creating and identifying growth opportunities and providing advisory services.

Her award-winning writing, photography, and graphic design have been published in books, magazines, newspapers, brochures, and advertisements. She is also a screenwriter and producer, as well as a developer of online educational courses. She loves cooking, adventure photography, and is an avid biker, hiker, and water-sports lover.

Her everyday motto for living is based on Helen Keller's quote:

"Life is either a daring adventure or nothing."

Ingram Content Group UK Ltd.
Milton Keynes UK
UKHW020615170323
418714UK00017B/231/J